What people are saying

Ra...

There are no shortages of misconceptions about The Morrigan. Perhaps even more so now that she is a popular figure in modern Paganism. Daimler untangles many of our modern assumptions about this power goddess and takes readers on a deeper exploration of her lore. Raven Goddess is an excellent resource for all those seeking the Great Queen.

Stephanie Woodfield, author of *Celtic Lore and Spellcraft of the Dark Goddess* and *Dark Goddess Craft*

Raven Goddess: Going Deeper with the Morrigan is an excellent follow-up to Daimler's 2014 Pagan Portals book The Morrigan: Meeting the Great Queens. It provides new and more complete translations of key source material, and it clears up some of the misinformation about the Morrigan from both inaccurate scholarship and from modern pop culture. It provides helpful guidelines for deepening your connections to the Morrigan, who is one of the most active Goddesses in our world today. Highly recommended for beginners, but the translations alone are worth the price of the book for anyone.

John Beckett, author of *The Path of Paganism* and *Paganism in Depth*

Pagan Portals

Raven Goddess

Going Deeper with the Morrigan

Pagan Portals

Raven Goddess

Going Deeper with the Morrigan

Morgan Daimler

MOON
BOOKS

Winchester, UK
Washington, USA

JOHN HUNT PUBLISHING

First published by Moon Books, 2020
Moon Books is an imprint of John Hunt Publishing Ltd., No. 3 East Street, Alresford
Hampshire SO24 9EE, UK
office@jhpbooks.net
www.johnhuntpublishing.com
www.moon-books.net

For distributor details and how to order please visit the 'Ordering' section on our website.

Text copyright: Morgan Daimler 2019

ISBN: 978 1 78904 486 7
978 1 78904 487 4 (ebook)
Library of Congress Control Number: 2019952865

A CIP catalogue record for this book is available from the British Library.

Design: Stuart Davies

UK: Printed and bound by CPI Group (UK) Ltd, Croydon, CR0 4YY
US: Printed and bound by Thomson-Shore, 7300 West Joy Road, Dexter, MI 48130

We operate a distinctive and ethical publishing philosophy in all areas of our business, from our global network of authors to production and worldwide distribution.

Contents

Other Celtic Titles by Morgan Daimler

The Morrigan
Meeting the Great Queens
978-1-78279-833-0 (paperbook) ~ 978-1-78279-834-7 (e-book)

Brigid
Meeting the Celtic Goddess of Poetry, Forge, and Healing Well
978-1-78535-320-8 (Paperback) ~ 978-1-78535-321-5 (e-book)

Manannán mac Lir
Meeting the Celtic God of Wave and Wonder
978-1-78535-810-4 (Paperback) ~ 978-1-78535-811-1 (e-book)

The Dagda
Meeting the Good God of Ireland
978-1-78535-640-7 (Paperback) ~ 978-1-78535-641-4 (e-book)

Irish Paganism
Reconstructing Irish Polytheism
978-1-78535-145-7 (Paperback) ~ 978-1-78535-146-4 (e-book)

Gods and Goddesses of Ireland
A Guide to Irish Deities
978-1-78279-315-1 (Paperback) ~ 978-1-78535-450-2 (e-book)

This book is dedicated to all of the people out there who look to the trí Morrignae for wisdom, guidance, or inspiration. May you find what you are looking for and always have strength for every fight.

With special thanks to Lora for all the hard work and effort at educating the community.
Tá tú maoin, a chara

Foreword

Daimler has done it again.

Look, folks, ye know I always recommend going to native sources, first and foremost, for all sorts of good and righteous reasons. It's an important thing you could - or even should - be doing, in order to be respectful and walk in Right Relationship with the culture you wish to gain from, to learn from.

Morgan's work is a notable exception. There simply isn't another non-Irish Pagan writer who stands in better relationship with the Gods and Ungods of Ireland, as far as I can see. Their existing body of work on Pagan topics is one I recommend, and indeed refer to and learn from myself, time and time again.

And now this.

Another book dedicated to the Goddess I work for. A companion and expansion to their excellent previous book *The Morrigan: Meeting the Great Queens*. This one truly opens up the information that is available on the Irish Goddess of Battle and Prophecy, shows how much more there is to Her, and Her sisters; in the lore and in the author's personal experience.

In this work you will find guidance to facilitate your own study of the source material. You'll find real information and clarity on what exactly is, and isn't, truly known about the Morrigan. You'll find out what she looks like, what colours and tools are associated with Her, and how to correctly spell Her name. You're going to learn about Her relationship with the Dagda, and the other Beings that move around Her stories. Daimler also breaks down Her involvement in one of the major sagas - the Battle of Moytura (Cath Maige Tuired), and goes on to examine the place of this Goddess in the modern world, and how to connect to Her here and now.

All in all, I know this book will become an invaluable reference work that I keep right at my desk at the Irish Pagan

School HQ, alongside so many of Morgan's other books. It is a fantastic addition to the few quality books and resources on this Goddess that I can wholeheartedly recommend.

Lora O'Brien, author of *A Practical Guide to Irish Spirituality: Sli An Dhraoi*, and *A Practical Guide to Pagan Priesthood*.

Preface

This book is intended as a follow up to the previous *Pagan Portals - the Morrigan* but may also be read as a stand-alone work.

I have been an Irish-focused pagan since 1991 and was dedicated to the Morrigan for over a decade. Although in the last three years my focus has shifted more fully to the Daoine Maithe she is still an important deity to me. After writing my previous book *Pagan Portals - the Morrigan* in 2014 I have long debated writing a follow up with a tighter focus on the Morrigan herself and which would tackle some common misconceptions about her in ways that, hopefully, will allow people to develop a deeper, stronger relationship with her.

In writing this I have drawn on many different sources and have carefully referenced and cited all of them. My own degree is in psychology so I prefer to use the APA method of citations. This means that within the text after quotes or paraphrased material the reader will see a set of parentheses containing the author's last name and date the source was published; this can then be cross references with the bibliography at the end of the book. I find this method to be a good one and I prefer it over footnotes or other methods of citation which is why it's the one I use. I have also included end notes in some places where a point needs to be expanded on or further discussed but where it would be awkward to do that within the text itself.

As I have said before in my previous book *Pagan Portals - the Morrigan* I do not think that the religious framework we use to connect to the Gods matters as much as the effort itself to honour the old Gods I think we can all do this respectfully and with an appreciation for history without the need for any particular religion. Whether we are Reconstructionists, Wiccans, or Celtic pagans all that really matters is that we are approaching our faith with sincerity and a genuine intention. To that end this book is written without any specific spiritual faith in mind, beyond polytheism, and it is up to the reader to decide how best to incorporate the material. My own personal path is rooted in witchcraft and reconstruction so that is bound to colour some of my opinions in the text, however, so the reader may want to keep that in mind.

Pagan Portals - Raven Goddess was written as a resource for seekers of the Morrigan specifically and offers both solid academic material and practical advice on connecting with her in a format that is accessible and designed to be easy to read, although it does contain a lot of academic references to older mythology. It is meant to be a follow up to the previous *Pagan Portals - the Morrigan* and take a deeper look into details of this fascinating deity.

For some people this book may be one step in a lifelong journey, an attempt to better understand or connect to a Goddess who is both easily accessible and maddeningly hard to comprehend. For others this book may simply provide another viewpoint of the Morrigan, her history, and modern beliefs and practices associated with her. In either case I hope that the reader feels that some value is gained from the time spent with this short text, getting to know the Morrigan in a deeper sense.

Introduction

The Morrigan is not only a complex deity but one who inspires great passion in people today and there are many different viewpoints of Her to be found. In my previous book I tried to maintain as much objectivity as possible and simply offer the best information I could at the time of who and what she was, as well as relaying information about deities closely connected to her; in this work I am trying to maintain that same level of quality but am taking a more subjective approach. This is the Morrigan through both study and my own experiences over the last 15 years or more.

The Morrigan is one of the most popular Irish goddesses and there is a lot of information to be found about her from a variety of sources. Despite this it can be very difficult to find solid resources about her as the material available is almost overwhelming in quantity now but ranges so widely in quality that trying to sort out the valuable from the dross becomes an enormous task. Misinformation abounds and is quickly repeated and then taken as fact. A great deal of in-depth study is required to sort out opinions from facts, modern invention from older myth, and misunderstanding or mistranslation from quality sources. It's all a bit dizzying especially for those just starting out.

The Morrigan shows up as only a small section in some books taking on the subject of the Irish or Celtic Gods more generally; in older pagan works it wasn't uncommon to find her barely a footnote in the text with a warning against any engagement. This almost phobic reaction to the Morrigan has shifted particularly in the 21st century and with that shift we see a proliferation of sources especially online. In the last decade or so there have been several good books that have come out on the market many of them aimed at offering readers a solid introduction to the Great Queen. My own *Pagan Portals - the Morrigan* had such an aim, but there is also Stephanie Woodfield's *Celtic Lore & Spellcraft of the Dark Goddess: Invoking the Morrigan*, Morpheus Ravenna's *Book of the Great Queen*, and Courtney Weber's *The Morrigan: Celtic Goddess of Magick and Might*. Each of these has its own unique approach and particular books will work better for people from different backgrounds.

As we connect to a deity and work with them and devote ourselves to them, we will find ourselves on a rollercoaster ride of experience and information. I have always found the best approach is to ground the two together, to look for sources to support my experiences and to embrace my experiences as an outgrowth of my deepening understanding. With that in mind as we move forward with this text, I want to include a blend of academic material and my own thoughts on the Morrigan. Whether you agree with everything I have to say or not I hope this will all serve as food for thought for you to develop your own relationship with her. Never stop questioning.

She speaks as often in poetry as prose, so let me end this introduction with this poem which I wrote years ago after the dream it describes:

I dreamed last night -
dream or vision or something more -
of ravens and bloody rivers,
hounds and horses coursing,
pounding hooves and howling voices,
Herself crying "Woe to those who flee!
Blood and battle is upon them!
The fight is upon you!
Stand your ground! Stand and fight!
Hard slaughter and a great victory!"
Her voice and the roaring of a river,
water and blood mixing,
and hounds and horses,

and riders armed and armored,
A feeling of panic and joy
of despair and ecstasy joined
twisting together in my gut
until I wanted to rush forward
into any danger, throw myself,
heedless, into madness and battle,
blades clashing, water rushing,
screams of war and death together,
ravens' wings tearing the air
My breath coming in gasps and gulps,
too winded to add my voice to the din,
but pushing forward, forward, further,
each step a success as earth
become mud as it mixed with blood.
And then, abruptly, the dream was gone
I woke to stillness.
No blood. No battle.
No death. No river.
But a yard full of black birds
their voices strident and discordant
singing to me of dreams and shadows
I moved through the day
expecting wings and warriors
the vision like a memory of feathers
which irritates and soothes simultaneously
and, again and again, ceaseless as the tide,
Or a fast flowing stream,
Her voice calling "Awake! Arise!"....

Chapter 1

Towards a Deeper Understanding

As we take our first step into a greater understanding of the Morrigan let us begin by seeking a better understanding of who she is and of things associated with her that are not discussed as often. In this chapter we will look at physical descriptions of the Morrigan in source material, colours connected to her, and her association with a more obscure item. All of this is presented for the reader to consider and weigh against their own experiences and opinions.

Description

A common question that I hear people asking is what does the Morrigan look like, so let's begin with that. There is, of course, a great deal of artwork to be found based in each artist's imagination but let's move past these modern conceptions to find a base to build outwards from. Looking at what we know from mythology and folklore we find a complicated answer. This is because generally when she appears in mythology she is not described in much detail. Instead we get passages like this one from the Cath Maig Tuired:

> The Unish of Connacht calls by the south. The woman was at the Unish of Corand washing her genitals, one of her two feet by Allod Echae, that is Echumech, by water at the south, her other by Loscondoib, by water at the north. Nine plaits of hair undone upon her head.

Similarly, when she appears in most versions of the Táin Bó Cúailnge[1] (TBC) it simply says *"Then came the Morrigan daughter of Ernmas from out of the Sídhe"* without adding any physical details.

There are a few appearances which are described however.

In the Táin Bó Regamna (TBR) we are given this:

> *A red-haired woman with red eyebrows was in the chariot with a*
> *red cloak around her shoulders; the cloak hung down at the back of*
> *the chariot and dragged on the ground behind her.*

This description of a red-haired woman[2] may be the most detailed description we ever get of the Morrigan's physical appearance and it is the only one where we are never told that she is in disguise or in an assumed form. In my own opinion this is most likely to be her true appearance, but other people may have different conclusions. In the Cath Magh Rath she is described as:

> *Bloody over his head, fighting, crying out*
> *A naked hag, swiftly leaping*
> *Over the edges of their armor and shields*
> *She is the grey-haired Morrigu*

This description is somewhat similar to another of the Morrigan's appearances in the TBC: "*then came the Morrigan daughter of Ernmas from out of the Sí shaped as an old woman*". However, this passage makes it clear this is not her natural appearance but a "*richt*", a guise, form, or assumed shape. The idea of the Morrigan taking on other shapes or disguises is a common one, and in fact in the Metrical Dindshenchas she is called "*samla día sóach*" (a phantom, the shape-shifting Goddess) making it clear that her form is fluid and changeable.

It is debatable whether or not the brief description of the Morrigan in disguise as "*Buan's daughter*" in the TBC reflects her true appearance or is, as with her form as an old woman, merely a disguise. In this passage, which does not occur in all versions of the TBC she is described as "*young woman with a garment of every coloring around her and a form fiercely beautiful on her*". Personally,

I'm a bit suspicious because of the phrase *"delb...furri"* that is "a shape...on her". It is possible that it's just an expression, or perhaps it could be an allusion to the fact that the Morrigan has assumed this alluring disguise as part of her attempt to trick Cu Chulainn, who has of course seen her red-haired form in the TBR previously.

She also has several animal forms which are described in the TBC as *"a smooth, black eel"*, *"a rough, grey-red [wolf] bitch"*, *"a white, red-eared heifer"* and in the TBR we see these forms echoed in her threats to Cu Chulainn: *"an eel"*, *"a blue-grey³ wolf-bitch"*, and *"a white, red-eared heifer"* as well as *"a black bird"*. In the Lebor na Huidre she is also described as taking the form of a bird *"the Morrigan, she in the likeness of a bird"*. It is interesting to note that most of these animal depictions come with a specific color.

The Morrigan is clearly capable of assuming many forms to serve her purposes, and we have descriptions of many of them. I have only touched on some here to illustrate what we generally know about her appearance. It may be that her true form is of a red-haired woman dressed in red, as we see in the TBR, but certainly she is not limited to that. She comes to us in many shapes and forms, through many guises and many means. Ultimately, she is what she chooses to seem to be to each viewer, whether that is black bird or white cow, naked hag or fiercely beautiful young woman. She is Herself.

Colors and the Morrigan

It's an interesting thing that many of us who follow, work with, honor, or are otherwise connected to the Morrigan tend to associate her with the colors red, white, and black. At first one may wonder why, as there isn't any straightforward text or piece of evidence that says 'the Morrigan's colors are such and such'. However, if we look at the total of the evidence, that is all the textual references that mention her and also mention color, we can see some patterns that may explain it.

Directly relating to the Morrigan we admittedly have only a few pieces of color related evidence, but we do have some.

From the Táin Bó Regamna:

"A red-haired woman with red eyebrows was in the chariot with a red cloak around her shoulders"
"... he saw that she was a black bird on a branch near him."
"I will be a blue-grey wolf-bitch then against you," she said.
"I will be a red-eared white heifer then," said she...

From the Táin Bó Cúailnge:

"...a smooth, black eel"
"...a rough, grey-red bitch"
"...a white, red-eared heifer"

From the Cath Mag Rath:

"She is the grey-haired Morrigu"

Additionally, we see Badb referred to repeatedly as 'red-mouthed' or 'the Red Badb', for example here in the Cath Maige Tuired Cunga: *"The Red Badb will thank them for the battle-combats I look on."*. In the Tochmarc Ferbe Badb is described as a 'white woman' or 'shining woman' and in the Destruction of De Choca's Hostel she is also said to be red-mouthed and pale. Black would be associated with her through ravens and crows.

Macha, has less blatant references to color so more guesswork is required. As Macha Mongruadh [Macha of the red-mane] she would seem to be associated with the color red, something we may also with less surety say due to her being called 'the sun of womanhood' in the Rennes Dindshenchas. Her association with skull could perhaps give us the color white for her, although that in itself is an assumption based on her explicit connection to severed heads and the wider Celtic cultural use of skulls. Black is easier as she is clearly connected to crows and ravens, and grey is also a color connected to her through the hooded crow and through the most famous horse known to be hers [before he was known to be Cu Chulainn's] the Liath Macha, literally 'Macha's Grey'.

All three of the Morrigans [Morrigan, Badb, and Macha] are said to take the form of hooded crows, birds which are black and light grey, and of ravens or crows more generally. In several stories including the Táin Bó Cúailnge the Morrigan is said to appear *"in the form of a bird"* and one may perhaps assume the bird here was meant to be understood as a hooded crow or raven. In the Sanas Cormaic they are called the *"three Morrigans"* and later *"raven women"*. In one version of the Aided Conculaind we are told *"And then came the battle goddess Morrigu and her sisters in the form of scald-crows and sat on his shoulder"*. The names Badb and Macha are also words in Irish that mean crows or hooded crows, reinforcing the connection between the Morrigan(s) and the color black as well as grey.

For the curious a quick summary of the color meanings in old Irish, beyond the actual colors:

- Black had connotations of dark, dire, melancholy, and was used to express intensity, something like the word 'very' in English.
- White represented purity, brightness, holiness, truth but also bloodlessness and was sometimes used to describe corpses. It was also a color in combination with red that was often used to describe Otherworldly animals.
- Red[4] was used to describe things that were bloody, passionate, fiery, fierce, proud, guilty (think red cheeks) also used as an intensive.
- Grey usually represents age, in the plural the word for the color means 'veterans'.

So, we can see that when color is mentioned in association with the Morrigan it is usually red or black, and slightly less often white or grey, and rarely blueish-green. I might suggest that people who associate red, black, and white with her are either consciously or subconsciously picking up on these patterns from her stories, particularly of the colors of her animal forms when contesting with Cu Chulainn in the Táin Bó Cúailnge which are black (eel), red (wolf), and white (cow), although the red/black/white pattern is not limited to that. Badb and Macha share these color associations in different ways, indicating that it is not the Morrigan as a singular being for which these colors are important but rather that all three Morrigans relate to them.

Fulacht na Morrigna

One of the mysterious things that the Morrigan is associated with is called the fulacht na Morrigna, literally the Morrigan's cooking hearth. A fulacht is a type of outdoor cooking hearth or pit; the smaller ones were named for the Fíanna but the larger ones for the Morrigan (RIA, 1870). These fulachta were associated both with large outdoor stone cooking hearths and with cooking spits, so interchangeably in the texts and academic material that one might assume the two were parts of a single whole. Specific types of wood were associated with the fulacht, particularly in the law texts with the fulacht fían, and these included holly and rowan (Ó Néill, 2003). One might note that one of Cu Chulainn's geasa was not to eat at a fulacht, and this is exactly what he ended up doing after encountering the three crones cooking on rowan spits at a fulacht who offered him hospitality - which he also had a geis not to refuse (Ó Néill, 2003).

We are given descriptions of the Morrigan's fulachts in the Yellow Book of Lecan:

The cooking hearth of the Morrigan is thus that is a portion of raw meat and enjoined of cooked meat and a small portion buttered and nothing melting from the raw flesh and nothing of it burnt by the cooking and at the same time together the trio on the spit.

And also, in a very early Scottish text (utilizing Old Irish) which describes both the Morrigan's fulacht and the Dagda's anvil excerpted here:

Cooking pit of the Morrigan is thus that is a wood wheel and wood axle between fire and water and an iron body and two people raise the wheel. Smoothly and quickly it went around. Thirty spits projected from it and thirty bars and thirty stakes. A sail on it, and a wonder its form when its bars and wheels were in motion. The Fulacht of the Morrigan very sharp edge of a smith. (Celt. Rev. viii 74; translation mine)

The cooking pit appears in a story recounted in the Agallamh Beg:

It was they who made for themselves a shelter there that night, and made a cooking place by them, and Cailte and Findchadh went to wash their hands in the stream.

"There is a cooking pit" said Findchadh, "and it has been long since its making."

"It is true, said Cailte, "and this is a cooking hearth of the Morrigan, and is not built without water." (RIA, 1870; translation mine)

Archaeological evidence supports the existence of these ancient fulachts which are found across Ireland, and some of the larger ones are considered fulachta na Morrigna with one known of at Tara and one in Tipperary (Martin, 1895). Ó Néill suggests that the fulacht was actually only the wooden portion of the cooking spit and that rather than a fire pit as we would imagine one it actually involved the use of heated stones for cooking (Ó Néill, 2003). He uses a description of the Fían utilizing a fulacht in Keating's Foras

Feasa ar Eirinn as well as archaeology to support this; in Keating's account the fulacht was used not only for cooking but also to simultaneously heat water for washing after a morning of hunting so that the warriors would be clean before eating (Ó Néill, 2003). This theory is intriguing and fits the evidence well, explaining why the Morrigan's fulacht was said to need both fire and water; the spits would be used for cooking meat over a fire while heated stones were taken and used to make the water suitable for bathing, as well potentially for boiling food. Since the wood and water would obviously be long gone the only hard evidence left behind would be exactly what we do find at the sites of ancient fulachts: cracked stones in pits that may have been dug to reach water[5] (Ó Néill, 2003).

Taking all of this evidence we may perhaps tentatively conclude that the Fulacht na Morrigna was a type of multipurpose outdoor cooking pit. Meat would be cooked on spits, possibly on a rotating assembly or wheel, and water might be heated for use. The smaller fulachts were named for the Fíanna but the larger, and apparently more complex, fulachts were named for the Morrigan.

The Morrigan's fulacht is also associated with blacksmiths:

Perhaps because he also forges weapons of death, the blacksmith is sometimes thought to possess supernatural powers. As we have seen the author of an 8th century hymn asks God for protection from the spells of blacksmiths. The supernatural aspect of this craft is indicated further by the special treatment of the blacksmith in the list of professions in Bretha Nemed toísech. In the case of other craftsmen, three necessary skills are listed, but in the case of the blacksmith, the author draws on pagan mythology: 'three things which confer status on a blacksmith" the cooking spit of Nethin, the cooking pit of the Morrigan, the anvil of the Dagda. (Kelly, 2005, page 63)

It may be in this case that it is the skill to create these items which is the measure of the smith's worth, but it is uncertain.

End Notes

1   Book of Leinster version.

2   Literally the text says "bean derg" a red woman, however in Irish this is how hair color is usually given. See Audrey Nickel's "Color Me Irish" blog post for more on this. https://www.bitesize.irish/blog/color-me-irish/

3   For those who are interested in the use of color in Irish material it's given here as glas, or literally green, but green which can be anything from a light green or blue to a blue grey.

4   There are actually multiple words for the color red in Old Irish; I am using 'derg' here which is the one most often used in the texts to describe the Morrigans, et al, however it is not the only red used so that should be kept in mind.

5   It is worth noting here that O Néill concludes based on the date of the archaeological fulachts that they significantly predate the written accounts and therefore that the fulachts were likely mere cooking pits; however this leaves open the question of how evidence supports the pyrolithic use of fulachts and medieval texts also hint at this use if there is in actuality no connection.

Chapter 2

Misinformation and Truths about the Morrigan

The more popular the Morrigan becomes the more misinformation proliferates about her or connected to her, so let's focus here on clarifying some things. These aren't personal opinions but facts from the Irish language and mythology. Keep in mind, however, that everyone makes mistakes when it comes to things coming from other languages and everyone can fall prey to bad information being shared around, especially if they haven't read or aren't very familiar with the source material. So hopefully this chapter will help correct some of the most common mistakes and misinformation that is often floating around.

Is The Morrigan a Goddess?

One thing that I've seen repeated both online and in at least one book is the assertion that the Morrigan is never called a Goddess in Irish mythology or sources, so let's begin with that.

The Morrigan is called a Goddess at least twice that I can think of offhand.

In the Metrical Dindshenchas, poem 49 Odras, which says:

[then] the wife of the Dagda came,
a phantom the shape-shifting Goddess.
...the mighty Mórrígan,
whose ease was a host of troops.

In the Tochmarch Emire we also have this:

In the Wood of Badb, that is of the Morrigu, therefore her proven-
wood the land of Ross, and she is the Battle-Crow and is also called

the woman of Neit, that is Goddess of Battle, because Neit is also a
God of Battle.

Looking at the original language of each quote it is clear that the word used is in fact "goddess": día in the first example and bandee in the second. Gulermovich-Epstein in *War Goddess* also mentions that we have at least one prayer to the Morrigan, for success in a cattle raid, further cementing the view of her as a deity. I am not entirely sure where the idea began that she is never called one in the source material, but as you can see it is untrue.

How Do You Spell Her Name?

Another thing that I've been seeing off and on is people spelling the Morrigan's name 'Mhorrigan' or 'Mhorrigu'. Outside of some very specific circumstances[1] when writing in Irish the Morrigan's name is NOT spelled with an initial 'Mh'. Unless you are an Irish speaker writing in Irish in the case that calls for lenition, please don't do this. Its grammatically incorrect and it looks really weird. Also, it would then be pronounced Worrigan (or Vorrigan I suppose, depending on dialect). Which is how I read it every time I see it.

On a related note, there's also something of a trend to spell her name 'Morrighan'. I think this may be a version from the middle Irish that somehow mainstreamed, so it is a legitimate spelling. But as with the example above the pronunciation would be different, closer to 'MORE-ree-(gh)uhn', with the gh a sound that's swallowed at the back of the throat. The modern Irish is Mór-ríoghain, pronounced like 'MORE-ree-uhn' with the g lost entirely. If all of that looks like either too much effort or too hard to process then stick with the Anglicized Morrigan (MORE-rig-ann) or the Old Irish Morrigan (MORE-rih-gahn).

If this all seems like a huge pain in the butt, well, sorry, but this is the deal when you are honoring a goddess from a foreign culture and another language. Spelling matters. Pronunciation matters, in relation to the spelling you are using.

Why 'The' Morrigan?

Speaking of names, the Morrigan is always referred to with the definitive 'the' before her name, unless she's being directly addressed like in a prayer. I've been seeing a tendency for people to drop this recently, and it's worth keeping in mind that in Irish culture and mythology she's always referred to as *the* Morrigan. It may help to keep in mind that her name translates to a title - either Great Queen or Phantom Queen, so try thinking that you are saying that. Does it feel weird in English to say "I honor Great Queen" or "My goddess is Great Queen"? Which is why we say the Morrigan, the Great Queen.

Are Falcons Her Animal?

The idea that the Morrigan is associated with falcons and rebirth: not in the mythology or Irish folklore. I've traced this one back to an online article from 2005 which as far as I can tell is the source for the belief, as well as the idea that she is a Goddess of rebirth (also not something from mythology). The article was one person's thoughts and opinions and was not in any way based on mythology, but rather the person's intuition which the author was very upfront about.

The Morrigan and Cu Chulainn

This probably deserves a section of its own because of the amount of related misinformation, and in chapter 5 we will look in more depth at some retellings of their interactions during the Táin Bó Cúailnge. However here are some quick bullet points addressing the more common points:

The Morrigan loved Cu Chulainn: Well, no, not in a romantic way, not that we have any proof of although she certainly had an interest in him. There is one story (which does not appear in every version of the Táin Bó Cúailnge but only a few later ones) where she appears to him in disguise as a king's daughter, and she does tell him that she fell in love with him 'upon hearing of' his fame. However, this is highly suspicious for multiple reasons. Firstly, she's in disguise for a reason, because they two of them had previously met and had a rather dramatic disagreement with each other (see the Táin Bó Regamna). You would think if she really loved him, she'd show up as her Goddess-y self and offer that. Secondly, she's showing up at a point where he's already refused one king's daughter (Ailill and Medb's) and is filthy and starving. There's really nothing going on there to make anyone feel romantic. He tells her he's in a bad way and not in a position to meet a woman; she replies that she will help him; and he says he isn't guarding the ford to earn a woman's arse. At which point she threatens him. Now if she was actually in love with him, as a goddess of battle, wouldn't she be pleased that he was putting honor and duty before pleasure? On the other hand if the whole point was to trick him or anger him she certainly achieves that.[2] She's also shown in her previous encounter with him in the Táin Bó Regamna that she's quite willing to lie to him as well as greatly annoy him, so this has much more of the feel of that to it than of any genuine profession of emotion.

The Morrigan offered Cu Chulainn sovereignty and he refused it or she denied it to him because he refused her: Again, from the same king's daughter story in the Táin Bó Cúailnge Let's be clear - she never offers him sovereignty. She also never offers to have sex with him, although that is implied by his responses. What she actually says is that she has fallen in love with him because of his fame and that she has brought her treasures and her cattle. Nothing about making him a king or anything like that. Could someone argue it's implied? Perhaps, however Cu Chulainn was not a candidate for kingship which the Morrigan would have known. According to the Lebor Gabala Erenn it was Cu Chulainn who broke the Lia Fal[3] because it did not cry out under him or his foster son. And when the stone that cries out under the next king, the stone that is an Otherworldly treasure, is silent under someone they are really, really not sovereign material. I'd also quickly point out that when Irish Goddesses show up as Sovereignty to offer kingship to people, they generally do so disguised as withered old hags asking for a kiss or sex, to test the person's fitness to rule, not as gorgeous princesses offering their possessions.

The Morrigan and Cu Chulainn had sex or had a child: definitely not in the existing mythology.

What Exactly Happened With The Morrigan and Dagda That Samhain?

The Morrigan and the Dagda's union at Samhain is another thing I often hear misinformation about. If there is one story in Irish mythology relating to the Morrigan that most people are familiar with it is probably the scene in the Cath Maige Tuired where the Morrigan and the Dagda meet at a river, join, and then plan their strategy for the coming battle with the Fomorians. There are several interpretations of this incident but possibly the most common are that it shows the Morrigan as a goddess of sex and that it is a case of the Dagda trading sex for victory. Basically, I hear people repeating the idea that the Dagda sought out the Morrigan before Samhain, before a big battle, and had sex with her in exchange for her promise to help fight in the battle and/or for battle advice. I have a feeling the misinformation here is coming from people who haven't read the actual account or aren't very familiar with it but are only aware that the incident occurs.

This is a complicated one and is going to take a bit to untangle. First let's look at the actual story:

The Dagda had a house at Glenn Etin in the north. The Dagda was to meet a woman on a day, yearly, about Samain of the battle at Glen Etin. The Unish of Connacht calls by the south. The woman

was at the Unish of Corand washing her genitals, one of her two feet
by Allod Echae, that is Echumech, by water at the south, her other
by Loscondoib, by water at the north. Nine plaits of hair undone
upon her head. The Dagda speaks to her and they make a union.
Laying down of the married couple was the name of that place from
then. She is the Morrigan, the woman mentioned particularly here.

Afterwards she commands[4] the Dagda to strip his land, that
is Mag Scetne, against the Fomorians, and told the Dagda to
call together the aes dana of Ireland to meet at the Ford of Unsen
and she would go to Scetne and injure with magic the king of the
Fomorians, that is Indech mac De Domnann is his name, and she
would take the blood of his heart and kidneys of his battle-ardor
from him. Because of that she will give to the gathered hosts the
blood in her two palms, striking, groaning, warlike by the Ford of
Unsen. Ford of Utter Destruction was its name afterwards because
of the magical injury done to the king. ~ Cath Maige Tuired
(translation mine)

Now it has been argued that she does this because he slept with
her, in a sort of trade, but let's take a closer look at a few things.
Firstly, this meeting is said to be *"dia bliadnae"* or on a day yearly,
which implies that the two meet every year about that time. We
have hints from other material that the Morrigan may be the
Dagda's wife, specifically the Metrical Dindshenchas:

the wife of the Dagda
a phantom was the shapeshifting goddess
...the mighty Morrigan
whose ease is trooping hosts
Metrical Dindshenchas: Odras (translation mine)

One might note that the same word *"ben"* [wife/woman] is used in
both the Dindshenchas and Cath Maige Tuired passages. Whether
or not we give that any weight, we should at least consider that

the two do have a connection outside this single story. So, we see a yearly meeting with two deities who are associated with each other outside of this story as well. They meet at a pre-arranged location where the Dagda finds the Morrigan straddling a river washing her genitals. The Dagda says something to her - about what we don't know. After making this union – giving the site its name of 'bed of the married couple' - the Morrigan tells the Dagda to strip his land, a common military ploy, in the place the Fomorians will be and to gather the armies of the Tuatha De Danann, and then promises to go out herself and destroy one of the Fomorian kings with magic, which she subsequently does, bringing back two handfuls of blood as proof. At no point does the story explicitly state that a deal is made between them, or that the Morrigan's actions are in any way a response to or payment for the Dagda's. We can say with certainty that she never makes an offer to him, although we do not know what he says to her when he first sees her.

My personal take on this is simple. The Dagda and the Morrigan meet every year and this particular year their meeting falls just before a major battle. After having sex, the Morrigan tells the Dagda exactly what he is to do and what she herself will be doing until he gathers the armies. Anyone who is married or in a long-term relationship should appreciate the interpersonal dynamics going on here.

Did the Morrigan grant her aid to the Tuatha De Danann in trade for the Dagda's attention? There's really no indication of that in the text. The Morrigan is a member of the Tuatha De Danann, daughter of Ernmas and Delbeath according to the Lebor Gabala Erenn, and had every reason to assist the Tuatha De without payment. We also need to keep in mind that before this meeting the Morrigan had already gone to Lugh and chanted a battle incitement to encourage him to rise up and fight, so she herself was clearly both in favor of the battle and already encouraging it and acting for the Tuatha De.

It's an interesting passage and full of important information about both Gods, but I think we need to be cautious in rushing to interpret it, especially through a modern lens. Instead I think we need to look at what's actually going on and being said, and what happens, and let the story speak for itself.

To summarize:

- the Dagda didn't seek her out, it was a yearly pre-arranged meeting at that location
- we have no idea what they discussed before having sex, only that they talked
- yes, they had sex, but according to the Dindshenchas they were married, and also in the text of the Cath Maige Tuired where we find this particular story it refers to the location this happened at as 'the bed of the married couple'. I realize most translations give it as Bed of the Couple but the exact word used, Lanamhou, is a version of a term for one of the legal states of marriage in Irish law.
- yes, the Morrigan did give the Dagda battle advice right after the sex and did aid the Tuatha De Danann by promising to weaken one of the opposing kings, but she had already been aiding them, specifically by singing an incitement to Lugh to encourage him to fight and prepare for the battle. Since she'd already acted on her own to help them before this it doesn't make sense to see this meeting between a married couple at a yearly tryst as some kind of pay-off for her to help her own people.

Basically, what we have is a yearly meeting of a married couple at a specific location, some marital sex, some martial advice, and some battle magic against a common enemy.

This is just touching on a handful of the most common bits of misinformation or errors that I tend to see. There are sure to be more, of course, and in the next chapter we will take a deep dive into the Morrigan's confusion with two other goddesses. I hope this helped to clear some things up.

End Notes

1 For example in the vocative case, but that doesn't apply in the vast majority of cases where I've seen people using this spelling in English.

2 There's also been some supposition by scholars that this entire scene was added later to explain her coming at him in three animal forms in the next scene, for those unfamiliar with her promise to do so in the Táin Bó Regamna. It is certainly odd that she threatens to do so in the TBR, then appears as Buan's daughter in the TBC only to make the exact same threat again, however this would make sense if it were a case of scribes duplicating a scene or trying to re-explain something, or even integrating material from a different oral source (all things that aren't uncommon).

3 After it didn't cry out under him Cu Chulainn struck the stone and it has remained silent ever since.

4 I'm translating itbert, which is a form of as-beir, as commands, although it has nuanced meanings. It can mean says or speaks, but in a sense of orders which I believe is what the Morrigan is giving here it means commands. It can also mean singing or chanting.

Chapter 3

Nemain and Morgen la Fey: Untangling Confusing Connections

It's impossible to discuss the Morrigan without also discussing a variety of other beings who are connected to Her. In *Pagan Portals - the Morrigan* I tried to do this by discussing the other goddesses who are often called Morrigan or conflated with the Morrigan. There are a couple however where the confusion runs particularly deep and is so often perpetuated in modern material that the older sources are buried or ignored. What I'd like to do here, as we continue our journey to know the Morrigan on a deeper level, is dig into two of the beings most often confused with the Morrigan herself and look at why that happens and also why we should be cautious about that line of thought.

Nemain, Goddess of War

If you ask most Celtic pagans to name the three Morrigans a good number of them, in my experience, will say Badb, Macha, and Nemain despite the fact that Nemain is never explicitly called the Morrigan or included with the other two anywhere in Irish mythology. I personally blame this one on the multitude of modern pagan books which blithely say that the above-named trio are the three Morrigans, however it can likely be traced back to Hennessey's 1870 book *The Ancient Irish Goddess of War*. Hennessey put a lot of emphasis on Nemain and included her with Badb and Macha in his discussion of the Morrigan in a way that I feel led to the later conflation of Nemain with the three daughters of Ernmas elsewhere called the three Morrigans.

The primary source we have for Nemain in mythology is the Táin Bó Cúailnge (TBC) and this is often the main evidence people point to in support of Nemain as one of the Morrigan.

The TBC material is pretty thin though and just shows her acting as a war Goddess, alone or with Badb. At one point in the story Cu Chulainn shouts and arouses the supernatural forces, after which Nemain appears: "*Co ro mesc ind Neamain (.i. in Badb) forsin t-slóg.*" (Windisch, 1905). [So that Nemain, that is the Badb, intoxicated the army there]. The equating of Nemain and Badb is common and can be found in multiple sources where the two names are treated as interchangeable, although as we shall see the two also appear together fairly often. In another recension of the TBC we see Nemain appearing with Badb and Be Neit, shrieking and terrifying the gathered army. Heijda suggests - and I agree - that is quite likely that instead of "*Badb 7 Be Neit 7 Nemain*" [Badb and Be Neit and Nemain] this passage should read "*Badb .i. Be Neit 7 Nemain*" [Badb that is Be Neit and Nemain] (Heijda, 2007). This is entirely logical as Be Neit rarely appears anywhere as an individual being and in the glossaries is usually equated with either Badb or the Morrigan, and sometimes Nemain. In point of fact the name Be Neit simply means woman or wife of battle and may be a general term used to describe war Goddesses rather than a proper name, which would also explain why in glossary entries she is so often immediately equated to another named deity. Towards the end of the TBC we see Nemain appearing alone in a similar occurrence:

> ...*so that Nemain brought intoxication upon the army there, falling in their armor and on the points of their spears and sword-edges, so a hundred warriors of them die in the midst of the encampment and at the side of that place a time of terror the cry carried from on high.* Windisch, 1905, translation mine).

This may be a repeat of the same behavior by Nemain, which would support her role as a war Goddess who brings terror and madness, but in fairness it could also be a scribal error where the same incident was doubled. In any event it is safe to say that in the

TBC Nemain is associated with a cry which causes terror in those who hear it, and brings such panic that people fall on their own weapons or kill their comrades.

Heijda favors the idea of Nemain as an alternate name for Badb or as a goddess paired with Badb separate from the Morrigan. In the Lebor Gabala Erenn we are told that Badb and Nemain are two wives of Net: *"Net son of Indui, his two wives, Badb and Nemain without falsehood "*. In another version we are told that it is Fea and Nemain who are his wives and that they are sisters, daughters of Elcmar: *"Fea and Nemain: two wives of Net son of Indui, that is two daughters of Elcmar of the Brugh"*. Due to this Heijda suggests that Fea may be the name of Badb in the same way that Anand is for Morrigu (Heijda, 2007). Macalister agrees, suggesting that Fea and Nemain represent an earlier twin-pairing which evolved into the grouping of Badb and Nemain; he also suggests that Badb became a dyad with the Morrigu before becoming a triplicity with Morrigu and Macha (Macalister, 1940). This would suggest an interesting evolution for Badb as a primary war Goddess who formed a pairing with her sister Nemain, who she shares a father with, in some areas and with her two sisters, Morrigu and Macha, who she shares a mother with, elsewhere.

In contrast Gulermovich-Epstein prefers to see Nemain as one of the Morrigan although indirectly connected. This argument uses several degrees of separation in different glossaries to connect the Morrigan to Nemain. An entry in Cormac's Glossary says Nemain is Net's wife and also called Be Neit – *"Net that is a God of battle. Nemain his wife. She is Be Neit"*. There are several versions of this, but all are fairly homogenous. Since Badb and the Morrigan are also called Be Neit elsewhere Gulermovich-Epstein argues that Nemain may be one of the Morrigan (Gulermovich-Epstein, 1998). Of course, this is highly problematic in that "Be Neit" may not be a name at all and could just mean "woman of battle" and as such could be applied to any war Goddess. There is an entry in O'Clery's Glossary "*Nemhain that is crow of battle [literally badb catha] or a hooded crow*" (Gulermovich-Epstein, 1998). But O'Clery is extremely late - 17th century - and it's hard to say at that point if his statement that Nemain was Badb is a corruption of earlier beliefs or legitimate, and also since "badb catha" isn't capitalized at all it is possible he didn't mean it as a name at all but was simply calling her "*a crow of battle*" as he follows it with "*or a hooded crow*".

O'Clery's Glossary also gives us "*Nemain, that is madness or insanity*[1]" Gulermovich-Epstein, 1998). Another entry in Cormac's Glossary gives us: "*Be Neit, that is Neit the name of the man. The woman Nemain his wife. They are a poisonous couple indeed*". In O'Mulconry's Glossary we are told: "*Red Nemain, that is heat of a fire, that is: red Nemain passion and the rest*". It is interesting that O'Mulconry associates Nemain with both fire and passion, adding a layer of depth to her usual associations. It is also quite interesting that he calls her "*Nemain derga*" - red Nemain - as this is a common name given to Badb who is called the red Badb and the red-mouthed Badb. Additionally, we know that Nemain was a magic worker for the Tuatha De Danann, listed with the other war goddesses: "*Nemain, Danand, Badb and Macha, Morrigu who brings victory, impetuous and swift Etain, Be Chuilli of the north country, were the sorceresses of the Tuatha De.*" (Banshenchus, n.d.)

Another fascinating tidbit about Nemain's character can be gleaned from a passage of the Lebor Gabala Erenn which is discussing several women of the Tuatha De Danann, including the two sovereignty goddesses, Banba and Fotla, Danann, the three Morrigans - Macha, Badb, and Morrigu - and Fea and Nemain:

Banba, Fotla and Fea,
Nemain wise in poetry,
Danand mother of the Gods.
Badb and Macha rich in wealth

Morrigan powerful in sorcery
They encompass iron-death battles
the daughters of Ernmas.

Overall it seems clear she was associated Badb and Fea and was called both Badb and Be Neit herself. She does often appear acting with Badb though, suggesting that when she is called Badb it is being used as a title, rather than that she herself is Badb. We know she was one of the sorceresses of the Tuatha De Danann and also that she was said to be wise in poetry and *"without falsehood"*, and Cormac's Glossary calls her poisonous. When we see her appearing in stories in an active role, she is a bringer of *"mesc"*, that is drunkenness, intoxication, and confusion which is directly associated with her terrifying cry. She is madness, insanity, frenzy, and perhaps the passion of battle. Whether or not she was one of the Morrigan, per se, she was without doubt a Goddess of war and battle, and strongly associated with Badb. It does seem likely when looking at the total of the gathered material that Nemain originally formed a war Goddess pair with Badb, as the two are often associated with each other and act together, and Nemain is given the title of Badb. Certainly, she has been considered one of the Morrigan grouping for centuries now and deserves a portion of the title in a modern sense, if only as one of the great Irish war Goddesses.

Why Is Macha Included as One of the Morrigans and Not Nemain?

Because of the modern confusion around Nemain and the regular inclusion of Nemain along with Badb and the Morrigan there is sometimes confusion about why Macha is included among the three Morrigan and Nemain isn't. I hope in the first section of this chapter we've covered why Nemain isn't the Morrigan and wasn't historically viewed as one of the three Morrigans. But because the question around Macha and Nemain is persistent today let's take a look at that as well.

The simple answer is that we know Macha is one of the three Morrigan because she is referred to explicitly as such in several of the glossaries and we know Nemain isn't because she is at no point in the source material called the Morrigan or one of the Morrigans.

The complicated answer is that while Macha's connection to the Morrigan is easy to establish and fairly clear - she is repeatedly referred to as one of the three daughters of Ernmas with the Morrigan and Badb, is listed as one of the three Morrigans with the same two sisters, and acts along with them in stories - Nemain's connection is more convoluted as we just discussed. We can clearly say that she is a war and battle goddess and that she acts in ways that are similar to what we see the Morrigan doing. She is also very closely tied to Badb, who is one of the Morrigan.

Badb and Nemain share similar epithets including 'red' and 'red mouthed' and Nemain is sometimes referred to as 'Nemain, that is the Badb' or 'Nemain that is the Badb Catha'. It is likely that Badb's name like the Morrigan is also a title but in this case, we can see the use of it applied to Nemain indicating their close ties to each other. Nemain is also referred to as Be Neit which may mean wife of Net[2] or woman of battle and is itself a name or title we see applied to other war goddesses. Nemain is said to be the wife of Net along with Badb in some sources, while others say she is his wife along with her sister Fea; unlike the three daughters of Ernmas Fea and Nemain are daughters of Elcmar. This is not a clear subject however, with some scholars like Heijda favoring the idea that Nemain is Badb's true name, while others like Gulermovich-Epstein seeing Nemain as one of the multitude of Morrigan goddesses but indirectly connected.

We can say with certainty that she is not one of the three if we are looking specifically at that triple grouping, but we can also say that she does appear together with Badb inciting battle and causing strife. While we can confidently include her among Irish war goddesses whether or not she is one of the Morrigan per se will probably always be an open question. On the other hand, Macha's place among the Morrigan is strongly established in the source material.

The Morrigan and Morgen la Fey

One source of much confusion is the connection - or lack thereof - between the Irish goddess the Morrigan and the Welsh Arthurian figure Morgen le Fay[3]. This is a subject that has been muddled in modern paganism for a long time and I won't deny that there are plenty of books out there that will directly contradict what I am about to say. People are very drawn to the idea that these two goddesses are connected or are the same being and it is an idea that many people are reluctant to reconsider. That said I am presenting here the source material and research I found when I investigated the potential historic connection between the two.

The short answer is historically there's no connection between the Morrigan and Morgen le Fay.

The Morrigan is an Irish goddess with complex associations to battle, war, death, prophecy, sovereignty, magic, incitement, and victory. Her name in older forms of Irish was pronounced roughly 'MORE-rih-guhn' and later forms 'MORE-ree-uhn' and meant either great queen or phantom queen, depending what etymology one favors. We have a wide selection of mythology and folklore featuring her and it's clear that when she shows up, she's an active force in whatever she's doing.

The Morrigan has two sisters, Badb and Macha, who she appears with in some myths usually performing battle magic; in the Táin Bó Cúailnge she also appears with Nemain and Be Neit for the same purpose. The Morrigan in later mythology would come to be associated with night terrors and specters, viewed as demonic because she could not easily be turned into a meek saint.

Morgen le Fay is a character first found in Arthurian stories, specifically the 12th century works of Geoffrey of Monmouth, where her name was initially spelled Morgen le Fay. It is worth noting that this spelling is significant because while both Morgan and Morgen are men's names (also worth noting) they are pronounced differently - Morgan evolved into the modern Welsh Morcant while Morgen became Morien (Jones, 1997). In the 12th century Morgen would have been pronounced, roughly, 'Mor-YEN' (Jones, 1997). The name Morgen is generally believed to mean 'sea born'.

Geoffrey was collecting local stories from Wales and publishing them in France and while he certainly didn't invent Morgen for his Viti Merlini there is no way to know for certain how much, or little, he shaped the character as he preserved her. Which in fairness is true for all of the Arthurian characters he wrote about. That aside however Geoffrey's Morgen was a priestess, one of nine sisters connected to Avalon. In the 15th century Morgen would be renamed Morgan by Thomas Malory and recast as King Arthur's scheming half-sister who was set against both Arthur and his wife Guinevere.

One of the main arguments connecting the names is that they sound the same to modern English speakers, but I hope it's clear here that in Irish and Welsh the two names sound very different. They also have different meanings and that is significant. Another argument that favors them being the same deity is that they are both connected to magic, but while one may argue that both do indeed practice enchantment the nature of the magic they practice seems to be vitally different and outside of that single similarity the rest of their associations are very different. Morgen is connected to healing and, perhaps, to guiding the dead or dying to Avalon or the Otherworld; the Morrigan is associated with death and battle but nothing in her mythology relates her to healing or to a role as a psychopomp[4]. People also argue that their stories have similar themes, but this is clearly not so. The Morrigan is married to the Dagda and may or may not try to seduce Cu Chulainn in one story while Morgen in various stories is married, is adulterous, and even tricks her own brother into conceiving a son with her. The Morrigan incites battles by directly encouraging people to rise up and fight while Morgen in some of her stories sows discord in more subtle ways. The Morrigan's main location is a cave, Uaimh na gCat, while Morgen's is an island on a lake, Avalon. These are only a few examples just to illustrate the very different natures of the two beings.

The Morrigan and Morgen le Fay are often associated with each other in modern paganism, perhaps because they are both perceived as powerful and potentially dangerous women who have gotten a bad reputation that they may not deserve. Both certainly were vilified and demonized over time as stories evolved, the Morrigan going from a goddess to a night specter and Morgen from a priestess of Avalon to an incestuous and usurping sister of the king. I certainly understand why people see associations between the two, although for myself I'd be more likely to picture them sharing stories at the bar over shots together than to believe they are the same being or energy.

I am aware of theories that Morgen was originally a Welsh goddess; I cannot say whether or not Morgen is a deity or ever was a deity, nor do I deny that someone does answer when people call on Morgen le Fay today. What I can say is that there's no evidence that the Morrigan and Morgen le Fay share any roots or that historically the two have any connection to each other.

End Notes

1 Dásach is a term which can mean fury, frenzy, violence; the related word dásacht is applied to rabid animals, but it can also mean ecstasy or war-like rage. It carries implications of a sudden uncontrolled fit of emotion.

míre is a form of mer and means demented, crazy, rash, but

can also be used in a positive sense to mean spirited or lively. It would be equally accurate to translate this passage as "Nemain, that is fury or terror" however I feel my translation uses the two words in a synonymous sense which seems to have been the intent of the original.

2 Net is an obscure war god.

3 I am aware that in modern terms her name is often given now as Morgan la Fey however I am choosing to go with the older original spelling used by the first person to write her name down.

4 See chapter 4 for discussion of modern myth relating to the Morrigan's connection to psychopomp activities and rebirth.

Chapter 4

The Morrigan's Role in The Cath Maige Tuired[1]

A key text of Irish mythology is the Cath Maige Tuired, a tale of war between the Tuatha De Danann and the Fomorians over the right to rule Ireland. One particular figure who appears repeatedly throughout the story is the Irish war goddess the Morrigan, yet her role in the text is often difficult to fully understand using existing English translations which omit significant amounts of her dialogue and, due to translation choices, in some cases give an imprecise impression of her actions. When the Cath Maige Tuired is looked at in full in the original language the Morrigan's role within the story takes on greater significance and nuances, which are otherwise lost, become clear. Taking each of her appearances in turn, with more literal translations, will show the importance of her actions in inciting the battle, using magic to fight against the Fomorians, and rallying the Tuatha De Danann to victory before finally offering a dual prophecy of the fate of the people to come.

To begin it must be understood that the Cath Maige Tuired (CMT) itself presents a challenge to translators, resulting in the current popular translations by Elizabeth Gray and Whitley Stokes both omitting passages, some of them lengthy. In a 2014 lecture by John Carey called "A London Library, An Irish Manuscript, A British Myth? The Wanderings of 'The Battle of Moytirra'" Carey traces the history of the only extant manuscript containing this vital Irish myth and discusses the unique difficulties it presents. One of the most important points in Carey's lecture is that the manuscript for the Cath Maige Tuired is believed by scholars to have been written by a younger scribe who was fond of intentionally obscuring his writing with:

...willfully eccentric orthography in which certain aspects of Old Irish, together with other usages which seem to be the fruits of pure fantasy, are deployed without rhyme or reason to produce a kind of Irish which looks like nothing else on earth. (Carey, 2014, p 8).

What this means in practical terms is that the Irish of the CMT is non-standard and sometimes impossible to fully relate to known words in either Old or Middle Irish. There are points where it is difficult to be sure what a word is supposed to be and others where it is left entirely to supposition. Perhaps this is why Stokes chose, even in the Irish, to omit passages entirely; Gray included the full Irish text however chose not to translate all of it. For my purposes here I have included my own translations of passages often omitted or not fully translated as they are pertinent to the Morrigan's role in the story; however expert linguists don't agree on what some of these words are so my translations should be understood as educated guesses and may be open to further interpretation[2].

Warfare for the Irish was a highly ritualized and structured affair and poetic incitement before battle was an established practice (Gulermovich Epstein, 1998). This incitement served to both demoralize the enemy and to inspire one's own side; in the Irish material this is manifested as laíded, incitement through inspirational speech, and gressacht, incitement through derogatory speech or insults (MacCana, 1992). The importance of such incitement, and its role in battle, cannot be understated. Both laíded and gressacht acted as essential forerunners to actual battle, ensuring that the individual or army was sufficiently motivated to fight to victory. Perhaps related to both of these are rosc catha, magical battle chants, which are also employed and, in many cases, may be identical to laíde in stories. The effect of the rosc catha and laíded in the stories are magical in nature but also appear to have a psychological aspect, in that they provide confidence and courage to the army being supported by them.

The first appearance of the Morrigan occurs after Lugh has

been accepted at Tara and initial plans for the battle against the Fomorians have begun. The Tuatha De Danann have separated for three years to prepare for the coming fight. The Morrigan goes to Lugh and incites him to battle, using a laíded as follows[3]:

Undertake a battle of overthrowing," so to the Gods sang the Morrigan turning to Lug, "Awake, make a hard slaughter, smiting bodies, attacks boiling, greatly burning, devastating, the people to a man crying out...

Looking at the full passage in Irish we see that the Morrigan is not merely urging Lugh to "awake" but to fight fiercely and mercilessly against the Fomorians. The intense tone seems meant to inspire and motivate him to equally strong action. Such an approach is typical of laíded, a practice which Proinsias MacCana likens to psychological warfare and can involve either demoralizing one's enemy or invigorating one's own forces (MacCana, 1992). It is important to note as well that this passage occurs directly after Lugh, accompanied by two champions of the Tuatha De Danann, the Dagda and Ogma, has gone to the three Gods of skill and been equipped with arms and armor specially prepared for the war and immediately before Firgol the druid gave a prophesy of the battle to strengthen the resolve of the Tuatha De Danann. This series of events could also fit with the ritualized approach to conflict to which the laíded could belong (MacCana, 1992). We see the Morrigan initially within this context as a force of incitement, setting things in motion and inspiring battle.

After Firgol's prophecy the Morrigan reappears, this time in a short passage where she is meeting the Dagda, relaying battle strategy, and magically attacking the Fomorian king Indech:

The Dagda had a house at Glenn Etin in the north. The Dagda was to meet a woman on a day, yearly, about Samain of the battle at Glen Etin. The Unish of Connacht calls by the south. The woman was at the Unish of Corand washing her genitals, one of her two feet by Allod Echae, that is Echumech, by water at the south, her other by Loscondoib, by water at the north. Nine plaits of hair undone upon her head. The Dagda speaks to her and they make a union. Laying Down of the Married Couple was the name of that place from then. She is the Morrigan, the woman mentioned particularly here.

Afterwards she commands the Dagda to strip his land, that is Mag Scetne, against the Fomorians, and told the Dagda to call together the aes dana of Ireland to meet at the Ford of Unsen and she would go to Scetne and injure with magic the king of the Fomorians, that is Indech mac De Domnann is his name, and she would take the blood of his heart and kidneys of his battle-ardor from him. Because of that she will give to the gathered hosts the blood in her two palms, striking, groaning, warlike by the Ford of Unsen. Ford of Utter Destruction was its name afterwards because of the magical injury done to the king.

This meeting is interesting in several ways. Firstly, this meeting is said to be *"dia bliadnae"* or on a day yearly, which implies that the two meet every year about that time. We have hints from other material that the Morrigan may be the Dagda's wife, specifically the Metrical Dindshenchas:

the wife of the Dagda
a phantom was the shape-shifting goddess
...the mighty Morrigan
whose ease is trooping hosts.

One might note that the same word *"ben"* is used in both the Dindshenchas and Cath Maige Tuired passages. Also, within this section of text in the CMT the term *"lanomhnou"* is used, which appears to be a variant of lánamna the genitive singular of lánamain which means married couple. Whether or not any weight is given to this, it is worth considering that the two do have a connection outside this single story. They meet at a pre-arraigned location where the Dagda finds the Morrigan straddling a river washing her genitals. The Dagda says something to her, but what is unknown. The two then make a union and the Morrigan tells the Dagda to strip his land, a common military ploy, in the place the Fomorians will be and to gather the armies of the Tuatha De Danann. She then promises to go out herself and destroy one of the Fomorian kings with magic, which she subsequently does, bringing back two handfuls of blood as proof. This action as described in the text involves the Morrigan going to the gathered army of the Tuatha De Danann with two palmfuls of blood which she then strikes while groaning. The word used, oconn, is also a term occasionally used for incitement, although much less frequently then laíded or gressacht. It is possible that a more accurate translation of that sentence might be *"Because of that she will give to the gathered hosts the blood in her two palms, striking, inciting, warlike by the Ford of Unsen."* If this is so then this is the second occurrence of the Morrigan actively inciting the army to battle, which as will become apparent may be one of her strongest themes in this story. Certainly, whether it is active incitement or inspiration through action her magical destruction of Indech and her public presentation of his blood to the army is meant to encourage her own side to victory.

The next appearance of the Morrigan is just prior to the battle, when Lugh questions the gathered Tuatha De Danann about what they will contribute to the fight:

"And you, oh Morrigan," said Lugh, "what ability?"
"Not hard," said she, "Pursue what was observed, pursue to strike down, I control bloody destruction."

Here the Morrigan, as in her promise to the Dagda to destroy Indech, is boldly proclaiming her own abilities. Although the word *"ar-rosdibu"* is cryptic if it is taken as an atypical compound word and broken down into ar ros dibu the meaning could be given as "bloody destruction" which is perhaps intended to echo her earlier delivery of Indech's blood to the hosts. In that case it becomes both a play on words and also a reminder of her previous attack on the Fomorian king. In this passage, unlike the others, there is no discernable battle incitement but the proclamation of her own prowess and dominion over that which she pursues is clear.

The two sides engage each other and the battle is not going in favor of the Tuatha De Danann. It is at this point that the Morrigan re-enters the story once again to incite the army, this time to turn the tide of battle and ensure victory.

Once again Stokes and Gray avoid the bulk of this material. Gray gives it simply as

Then the Morrigan the daughter of Ernmas came, and she was strengthening the Tuatha De to fight the battle resolutely and fiercely. She then chanted the following poem: "Kings arise to the battle! (Gray, 1983).

Similarly, Stokes offers it as:

Then the Morrigan, daughter of Ernmass, came, and was heartening the Tuatha Dea to fight the battle fiercely and fervently. So then she sang this lay below: 'Kings arise to the battle', etc. (Stokes, 1891).

This is unfortunate because while the language is difficult and obscure it is evocative. My own translation:

Next the Morrigan daughter of Ernmas came, and urged the Tuatha De Danann to give battle stubbornly and savagely. So that in that place she chanted her incitement down: "Arise, kings to battle here! Seizing honor, speaking battle-spells, destroying flesh, flaying, snaring, seizing battle ---, seeking out forts, giving out a death feast, fighting battles, singing poems, proclaiming druids collect tribute around in memory. Bodies wounded in a rushing assault, pursuing, exhausting, breaking, prisoners taken, destruction blooms, hearing screams, fostering armies battle, occupants moving, a boat sails, arsenal cuts off noses. I see the birth of every bloody battle, red-wombed, fierce, obligatory-battlefield, enraged. Against the point of a sword, reddened shame, without-great-battlements, preparing towards them, proclaiming a line of battle Fomorians in the chanted margins, helpfully impels a reddened vigorous champion, shaking hound-killing warriors together, bloody beating, ancient warband towards their doom.

As with her earlier incitement of Lugh, the full text makes it plain that the Morrigan is not merely urging the kings to "arise to battle" but rather to arise and fight to the destruction of their enemies. This is clearly a type of laíded and indeed while the verb used is rocachain, a form of canaid, "sing or chant", the noun is "laíd-se" which in context I am translating as "her incitement". When laíded are used in other material, such as the Táin Bó Cuailnge, they normally occur with the verb form (MacCana, 1992). This may be a way to emphasize to the audience that incitement is occurring before the actual poetic speech is presented, and in this case the use of the noun form of the word could be another play on words. Her goal of incitement is achieved as her words spur the Tuatha De Danann to turn the tide of battle and achieve victory.

Several small incidents occur at the end of the battle including the now-deposed king Bres bargaining with Lugh for his life and the Dagda pursuing his harper who has been taken by the retreating Fomorians. The Morrigan's final appearance, indeed the end of the story as we have it, occurs after the carnage has been cleared away when the gathered Tuatha De Danann call on the Morrigan and ask if she has any news and she replies with two poems. The first is a prophecy of peace.

Although this prophecy is one of the most well-known of

the Morrigan's dialogues, Gray translates only the first eight lines and Stokes only the first four. Both found the remaining text too obscure to attempt to translate, with Stokes ending the fourth line with "etc.," and Gray inserting "gap; meaning of text unclear" (Stokes, 1891; Gray, 1983). The following is my own understanding of the full poem:

After the defeat at the battle's end and the clearing out of the carnage, the Morrigan daughter of Ernmas arrived to announce the deaths of the battle there, and the mighty victory done there to the fair knights of Ireland and beings of fairy-swords, and beings of proud waters, and beings of abounding rivermouths. Thus, that Badb recounts great exploits still. "Have you any story?" They all turned towards her there mentioned before.

"Peace to sky.
Sky to earth.
Earth below sky,
strength in each one,
a cup overfull,
filled with honey,
sufficiency of renown.
Summer in winter,
spears supported by warriors,
warriors supported by forts.
Forts fiercely strong;
banished are sad outcries
land of sheep
healthy under antler-points
destructive battle cries held back.
Crops [masts] on trees
a branch resting
resting with produce
sufficiency of sons
a son under patronage

on the neck of a bull
a bull of magical poetry
knots in trees
trees for fire.
Fire when wished for.
Wished for earth
getting a boast
proclaiming of borders.
Borders declaring prosperity
green-growth after spring
autumn increase of horses
a troop for the land
land that goes in strength and abundance.
Be it a strong, beautiful wood, long-lasting a great boundary
'Have you a story?'
Peace to sky
be it so lasting to the ninth generation

This prophecy of peace is followed immediately by a second prophecy, with a much grimmer tone:

She was afterwards among them prophesying the years at the end of existence, and further promising each evil and lack in those years, and every plague and every vengeance: so that there she chanted her poem:

Something seen is a world that shall not be pleasing: summer deprived of flowers, cows deprived of milk; women deprived of modesty, men deprived of valor. Conquests without a king, pointed, bearded, mouths of many-oaths, sorrow, a lord without judgments. Sea without profit. Multitude of storms, excessively tonsured, forts, barren of structures, hollow, a stronghold coming from mistakes a devastated time, many homeless, an excess of lords, joy in evil, a cry against traditions, bearded faces. Equipment decaying, numerous exploits, finding battles, silent towards a spurred horse, numerous assemblies, treachery of lord's sons, covered in sorrow, crooked judgement of old men. False precedents of judges, a betrayer every man. A reaver every son. The son will go lay down instead of his father. The father will go lay down instead of his son. In-law each to his own kinsman. A person will not seek women out of his house. A long enduring evil period of time will be generated, a son betrays his father, a daughter betrays [her mother][4]

Looking at the two poems together provides insight not only into the Morrigan as a prophetess but also demonstrates basic features of what the Irish at the time considered good and bad conditions to live in. In the first prophecy peace is all encompassing, extending from sky to earth and the world is full of plenty in all ways. Borders are strong and secure, sad cries and battle cries are gone, and the land has strength and abundance. In contrast the second prophecy offers a vision of the exact opposite: lack in all important areas, discontent and dishonor, false judgements, and rampant incest. Unfortunately, the manuscript ends abruptly in mid-sentence, making it impossible to guess how the prophecy would have ended.

The Cath Maige Tuired is an important mythological text which provides a great deal of information about the Irish gods and their early time in Ireland. One of the most significant of these gods is the Morrigan who plays an essential role in the rebellion against the Fomorians using both her own magical power and the poetic form of laíded. The Morrigan repeatedly appears in the story to incite the Tuatha De Danann to battle with obvious good effect. These acts of incitement all occur at pivotal points where her involvement seems crucial to ensuring victory: she appears to incite Lugh to fight after he is armed, she appears to the gathered army *"groaning, warlike"* after a pledge to destroy the Fomorian King Indech, and finally she appears at the turning point of the battle to incite the Tuatha De Danann to rise up and claim victory. In each case her incitement is strongly worded, direct, and relentless. She promises to use magic to injure the Fomorian king Indech by taking his battle ardor, bring back two handfuls of his blood to the gathered army, and Indech is later overcome and killed in the final battle, almost certainly as a result of the Morrigan's battle magic. At the end she prophecies a positive and negative fate for the world, having ensured victory for her own side. Looking carefully at the Irish text and literal translations of the text it becomes plain that the Morrigan is a driving force in the battle, both through incitement and active participation. It is perhaps fitting that the extant text ends with the Morrigan's words of prophecy, as she played a vital role in instigating and ensuring the outcome.

End Notes

1 This section was originally published as an article titled 'The Role of the Morrigan in the Cath Maige Tuired: Incitement, Battle Magic and Prophecy' in Air n-Aithesc vol. II, issue II, August 2015. What appears here is a modified and edited version.

2 Isolde Carmody of Story Archeology has also given versions of some of these which can be found here: https://storyarchaeology.com/the-morrigan-speaks-her-three-poems-2/
I encourage people to read the different versions to compare them, as this can help give a better understanding of the overall feel of the material.

3 This passage is particularly difficult to translate, and neither Stokes nor Gray give a full version of it. This may be understandable as the text following the initial sentence is difficult and presents issues typical of the problems endemic in the CMT, however what I am offering here is my own understanding of the passage.

4 The existing manuscript of the Cath Maige Tuired ends with

the line 'a son betrays his father, a daughter betrays' but it seems logical to extrapolate that the sentence would finish 'her mother' if we had the following page.

Chapter 5

Re-telling the Ulster Cycle: The Morrigan and Cu Chulainn

There is possibly no subject relating to the Morrigan that causes more confusion or contention than that of the relationship between the Morrigan and Cu Chulainn. In the modern pagan community new myths and stories are growing relating to these two and new approaches to understanding them; I am not trying to tell anyone what to believe here. What I do want to do however is clarify what the older source material has to say because I understand that not everyone reads this material directly themselves or is familiar with the older stories.

For those who haven't read the Ulster Cycle consider this a slightly abridged re-telling of the Morrigan's interactions with Cu Chulainn, beginning with the encounter that sets up their encounters in the Táin Bó Cuailigne. These section focuses on the incidents in these stories where the Morrigan and Cu Chulainn interact to show the nature of their relationship across its course; however I am not including every single interaction they have across all mythology, rather I am focusing on the Táin Bó Cúailnge, one rémscel [pre-tale] the Táin Bó Regamna, and the Aided Cu Chulainn.

In the Táin Bó Regamna

Cu Chulainn wakes up to the sound of a cow bellowing. Leaping out of bed naked he runs outside with his wife Emer chasing him carrying his clothes. He yells to his charioteer, Laeg, to ready their chariot and they go to find out what all the hubbub is about. After a short ride they come upon a strange sight: a chariot pulled by a one-legged red horse, with the chariot post affixed through the horse's body and forehead. In the chariot is a red-haired woman wearing a red cloak which trails to the ground; next to it is a large man using a hazel rod to drive a cow who is bellowing.

Cu Chulainn points out that the cow doesn't like the way she's being driven and the woman replies that its none of his business because it's not his cow, or his friend's cow. Cu Chulainn then says that it is his business because every cow in Ulster is his business, to which the woman replies that he takes on a lot. He then asks why she is talking to him and the man isn't and she says because she's the one he yelled at. He then says that when she speaks, she speaks for the man and she replies by giving the man's name as "Cold wind-conflict-brightness-strife". Cu Chulainn remarks that this is a wondrous name and asks if she is going to speak for him the whole time and what her name is, at which point the man speaks, and tells him that the woman's name is "Keen edged-small lipped-plain cloaked-hair-sharp shouting-fierceness-a phantom"

Cu Chulainn gets angry at this point and accuses them of trying to make a fool of him, then leaps onto the woman in the chariot and holds a spear to her head, asking her who she really is.

She tells him that she is a satirist and that the cow was payment for a poem, given to her by Daire mac Fiachnai of Cúailnge So, Cu Chulainn says that he wants to hear her recite a poem and she says she will if he will get off of her, which he does, jumping down between the chariot poles.

She proceeds to recite a poem against him and he leaps into his own chariot only to find that the woman, cow, and man have disappeared and only a black bird remains perched in a tree nearby.

He calls her a hurtful woman and she says that the place they are at will be named 'Bog of Distress' because of his words.

He says if he knew who he was talking to they wouldn't have parted that way and she pledges that whatever he would have done it would still have ended badly for him. He then says that she has no power over him, to which she replies that she does indeed, and that she is bringing and will bring his death; she then explains that she has brought the cow from out of the Sidhe of Cruachan to be bred by the Brown Bull of Cúailnge and that the calf it carries will start a great cattle raid, and implies that Cu Chulainn will die in this raid. He of course replies that he will not be killed and that he will become enormously famous in this cattle raid.

She then promises to wait until he is fighting a skilled opponent, who is his equal in all ways, and then she will come to him as an eel in the ford to trip him so that he will be fighting an unfair fight. He replies that he will dash her against a stone to break her ribs and that she won't be healed unless he himself blesses her.

She then promises to come at him as a wolf and tear a strip from his arm during the fighting so that the odds will be really unfair, to which he replies that he will wound her eye with his spear and she won't be healed until he blesses her.

Finally, she says she will appear as a red-eared white heifer driving fifty other cows before her into the ford and the fight will be so unfair that he will be killed and his head taken as a trophy. He pledges to break her leg with a sling stone and that she won't be healed unless he blesses her, which he will not do.

The two then go their separate ways.

The Táin Bó Cúailnge

The big cattle raid that the Morrigan predicted in the Tain Bo Regamna has now come to pass. In this part we are going to look only at the actions of the Morrigan in dealing with Cu Chulainn - keep in mind though this is not her only appearances in this story, nor even her most important ones in my opinion.

We begin with the story of King Buan's Daughter, but here's the thing about that: (1) it only appears as far as I know in one recorded version of the Táin Bó Cúailnge, (2) it is basically a modified and condensed version of some of the events in the Táin Bó Regamna which is older, specifically the threats to attack Cu Chulainn; some scholars have suggested this episode was added later by a scribe trying to justify the Morrigan's interaction with Cu Chulainn within the text and (3) I would highly advise taking the events with a huge grain of salt as we know that the Morrigan has previously been deceptive towards Cu Chulainn. I personally don't think the proclamation of love or offer to help him are genuine, but you can decide for yourself.

King Buan's Daughter

Cu Chulainn was guarding the ford after many long days fighting when he saw a beautiful young woman approaching. He asks her who she is and she says that she is the daughter of King Buan, and that she fell in love with him after hearing of his glorious deeds and has brought her treasure and her cows with her. He tells her it's not a good time, and that they are struggling and hungry so he isn't in a good position to meet a woman. She says that she could help him, but he replies *'I am not here for a woman's ass'*.

She then promised to cause him trouble by coming against him when he is fighting, tangling his legs in the form of an eel. Cu Chulainn replies that he prefers that to the King's daughter and says he will break her ribs and she will not be healed unless he blesses her. She then said she will drive cattle at him while in the form of a wolf to which he replies that he will smash her eye with a stone from his sling and she won't be healed unless he blesses her. Finally, she says she will come at him in the form of a hornless red heifer, and he says that he will break her legs with a sling stone and she won't be healed unless he blesses her. Then they part ways.

The Death of Loch

Cu Chulainn found himself fighting against the warrior Loch who was a formidable opponent and while they fought in the river ford the Morrigan came from the sidhe to fulfill her promise to destroy Cu Chulainn. She came in the form of a white red-eared heifer with fifty white cows, each bound to another with a bronze chain. Cu Chulainn threw a stone with his sling and broke one of her eyes.

Then she came at him again, this time in the form of a black eel who twined around his ankles and tripped him, so that he fell and Loch wounded him in the chest. Cu Chulainn rose when he was wounded and smashed the eel against some rocks, breaking its ribs.

Finally, she came at him as a grey-red wolf bitch, driving cows before her, and she bit him and distracted him so that Loch wounded him again this time in the loins. Cu Chulainn cast a spear at her and wounded her a third time, and was so enraged that he cast the Gae Bulga at Loch, impaling him upon it and mortally wounding him. Dying Loch asked that Cu Chulainn grant him the dignity of dying on his face not his back so that everyone would know he had not died trying to run away, which Cu Chulainn did.

Cu Chulainn then composed a poem of the fight in which he recounted the events, and mentions the wolf and eel attacking him, calling the Morrigan 'Badb'.

The Healing of the Morrigan

After fighting Cu Chulainn has what may fairly be called a very bad day, with Medb violating the agreement of fair combat which dictated that warriors would fight one on one by sending six warriors at once against Cu Chulainn.

The Morrigan then appeared again to Cu Chulainn disguised as an old woman[1] who was milking a three-teated cow. Because he had wounded her and no one could be healed from such wounds unless Cu Chulainn blessed them.

Desperately thirsty Cu Chulainn begs the old woman for a drink and she gives him some milk from the first teat. He responds by saying *"May this be a cure for me, O old woman"* and so the Morrigan's eye was healed. He begged for another drink and she gave him milk from the second teat to which he said *"May she be healthy now who gave this"* and her ribs were healed. He begged a third drink and she gave him one from the final teat, after which he said *"blessing of the Gods and un-Gods on you, woman"* at which her leg was healed. And so the Morrigan was healed.

Medb then attacks him again with her warriors and he defeats them

The Death of Cu Chulainn

Rounding out our modern re-telling of the Morrigan's interactions with Cu Chulainn we have what may be called the final chapter of the Ulster Cycle, the Death of Cu Chulainn. I will say this, there is some disagreement about some of the details here, specifically in some places who was doing what, and there are multiple versions of this story. I am giving a re-telling which I feel is true to the spirit of the originals, but of course I encourage everyone to read the originals themselves

The cattle raid of Cúailnge was done and over and Cu Chulainn had several other adventures since that time, but he had made some dangerous enemies, one of which was Queen Medb who had never forgiven him for ruining her plans to take the Brown Bull, or for killing so many of her champions. And she probably still remembered that time he killed her pets sitting on her shoulder when he flung a sling stone at her, as well. So Medb had gotten together many warriors who also hated Cu Chulainn, and she had gotten the children of Calatin, a warrior Cu Chulainn had killed in the Táin Bó Cúailnge to ally with her against him. The daughters of Calatin were fearsome looking, each having only one eye, and Medb sent them to be trained in witchcraft.

Medb began attacking Ulster again with her army and her new champions, hoping to draw Cu Chulainn out to fight.

Initially the people who cared about Cu Chulainn tried to trick him into not joining the fighting in several ways, including sending him to a valley where he would be unable to hear any outside noises, but he still saw the smoke rising from the other army and insisted on fighting.

The night before his final battle the Morrigan broke his chariot, trying to prevent his going because she knew he would not return. When he tried to leave the next morning there were several ill omens, including the weapons falling from the racks and Cu Chulainn's own brooch pin falling and cutting his foot. When he called for his chariot to be readied Laeg replied that for the first time his horse, the Grey of Macha was refusing to be harnessed. Cu Chulainn went out himself and spoke to the horse, who turned his left side to his master three times then cried tears of blood at his feet.

All the women wept to see him going, and after he left, he saw a woman [the Morrigan or Badb] washing bloody clothes in a river. When he called to her and asked whose clothes she was washing she responded that it was his own.

Then he came upon the three one-eyed daughters of Calatin disguised as three crones. They were at a cooking hearth by the side of the road cooking a dog on a rowan spit, and Cu Chulainn had geasa on him not to eat at a wild cooking hearth or to eat his namesake so he tried to hurry past. The three witches called out to him though and asked him to join them, and when he refused, they mocked him for turning down their hospitality saying he would have stopped for a grand meal but not for the small bit they had to offer. Since there was also a geis on refusing hospitality Cu Chulainn was literally screwed if he did and screwed if he didn't, so he stopped. One of the women offered him the shoulder of the cooked dog with her left hand and he took it in his left hand and ate, then put the bone beneath his left leg; the arm and leg immediately weakened.

Then he came to the plain of Muirthemne where the warrior

Erc has set up an ambush for him, with many warriors waiting. And it had been said that kings would fall by Cu Chulainn's spear so they had devised a clever strategy to get him to give them his spear, that is they set up three pairs of men fighting each other and with each stood a satirist. As Cu Chulainn went across the plain fighting the army he came upon the first pair of fighting men and the satirist called to him to stop them, so he did by killing them. Then the satirist asked for his spear, and when Cu Chulainn refused the satirist said he would make a mockery of him for not giving it so Cu Chulainn hurled his spear through the man. Then his enemies, Lugaid and Erc, recovered it and Lugaid asked the sons of Calatin who would be killed by the spear and one replied that a king would be killed by it. So Lugaid threw it and struck Laeg, who was acclaimed as the king of charioteers. Laeg died and Cu Chulainn carried on, removing the spear and driving his own chariot.

Then he came upon the second pair and again was asked to stop them, again killed them and had the satirist demand his spear. Again, he refused and the satirist said he would mock him but Cu Chulainn said he had already bought his honor that day, so the satirist promised to mock Ulster if he did not so he threw it through the man and this time Erc recovered it. He asked the sons of Calatin who would be killed by the spear and they replied a king so Erc threw it and mortally wounded the Grey of Macha who was called the king of horses. Cu Chulainn pulled the spear out and the Grey of Macha broke free and ran to the Sliab Fuait with half the yoke still attached.

Again, he drove across the plain and this time saw the third pair fighting and again stopped them when requested and as before the third satirist asked for his spear. He refused and the satirist said he would mock him but Cu Chulainn said he had already bought his honor that day, so the satirist promised to mock Ulster if he did not and he said he had paid for that already as well. Finally, the satirist promised to mock his whole people and Cu Chulainn threw the spear butt first through the man. Lugaid recovered it and asked the sons of Calatin who the spear would kill. They said a king, so as Cu Chulainn drove again through the army Lugaid threw the spear, disemboweling the king of Ireland's heroes. His second horse broke its yoke as well and fled, stranding the chariot with Cu Chulainn in it.

Now he asked his enemies if he could go to the nearby lake for a drink and they agreed as long as he promised to come back, and he said he would or if he could not, they would have to come get him. And he held his guts to his chest with his hands and went to get a drink, and wash himself, and prepare for death. On his return to the plain he saw a great pillar stone and he tied himself to it so that he would die on his feet. When his enemies gathered around him, they did not know if he was alive or dead yet, and as they waited the Grey of Macha came back and defended him for as long as he lived.

Finally the Morrigan and her sisters came in the guise of hooded crows and perched on the pillar, or some say on Cu Chulainn's shoulders, and so his enemies knew that the life was gone from him and they closed in to claim their battle trophies, carrying off his head and right hand to Tara, although Lugaid lost his own right hand when Cu Chulainn's sword fell and severed it.

Cu Chulainn's allies were hurrying to the plain and they met the Grey of Macha on the road, covered in blood and gore, and knew that Cu Chulainn had died. And they followed the horse to his body, where the Grey of Macha stood and laid his head against Cu Chulainn's chest in grief.

End Notes

1 I just want to note the Irish used actually specifies a woman over 70 years old.

Chapter 6

Ancient Goddess in The Modern World

One of the challenges with a deeper understanding of the Morrigan is finding a way to conceptualize her in the modern world and also to relate to some of her purviews in a modern way. What I often see is people trying to force the Morrigan into roles that don't suit her nature rather than trying to understand her nature and how she would organically find a place in modern paganism. In this chapter I want to look at some of the main areas where we find this, including how we understand sovereignty, and the Morrigan as a mother or sex goddess. With all of these I'd like to challenge readers to set aside preconceived notions and contemplate the ideas being presented with an open mind.

The Morrigan and Sovereignty

We talk a lot about goddesses of sovereignty, especially in Irish polytheism, but there is a disconnect between the ancient understanding of what those goddesses did and what they are seen to do in a modern context. Often the way that sovereignty is perceived is heavily colored by modern ideals of the value of the individual and of individual freedom, while the ancient view saw sovereignty as the right of one person to exert control over others. This disconnect is born from a misunderstanding or romanticism of the historic concept and yet may also represent a way in which the old gods are evolving and adapting to a new world.

To begin, sovereignty itself may not be a very good translation of the Old Irish word flaitheas, although it is one given by the dictionary. Flaitheas more properly should probably be translated as "rulership" or the right to rule, which is also another of its meanings. The ancient goddesses of sovereignty gave the kings and chieftains the right to rule over the people, effectively legitimizing their kingship. To have the blessing or approval of the goddess of sovereignty, to symbolically marry her, was to be given the divine right to rule. In the context of ancient Irish culture this was a very important thing because only with the approval of this goddess, only with flaitheas, could a king prosper in his rule; through right relation to the goddess of flaitheas a king could bring abundance and security to his people and land. Angering her though would lead to destruction, one way or another.

Where this gets tricky linguistically is that the word sovereignty in English not only means the authority of someone or something over a group, but also freedom from external control. While the Old Irish word means ruling, and is even used as a word to mean a kingdom or realm, the English word only partially overlaps these meanings and includes connotations of independence and freedom that are entirely lacking in the Irish. In this case the choice of words in translation is very important, especially since the newer understanding has grown largely out of the concepts surrounding the English term, not the Irish.

We live in a world where we are disconnected from the idea of sovereignty, in part because the modern idea is far different from the ancient one. Several Irish goddesses were bestowers of flaitheas, deciding who would rule over the geographic area they were associated with, such as Macha in Armagh or Aine in Limerick. A king or chieftain successfully rule over the land and people of his domain was dependent on the blessing of this goddess. Sometimes the king would ritually marry the goddess to symbolize his union with her, in other cases she would appear and offer him a drink from a cup representing sovereignty. It was very important that the king live in right relation with the goddess of sovereignty because to do so would bless his people with abundance and prosperity, while offending her or angering her would bring about loss and scarcity.

Many people today when they see the word sovereignty

used interpret it not as the right to rule a place and its people but rather as a word relating to personal autonomy. This may be inaccurate in a historical context, but for those of us living in a place without a functioning monarchy what else would sovereignty be? When there is no king to marry the land, no chieftain to be chosen and blessed by the goddess, then what becomes of the concept of sovereignty itself? How can we internalize it and make it personal, make it about our right to rule over our own land, which is our body, our own kingdom, which is ourselves. When we honor the goddess of sovereignty in our lives, we are honoring a modern concept of sovereignty, but that is no less impactful or important than the ancient one. It is different, and more personal, but just as powerful in its own way to call on a goddess of sovereignty today as ever.

The Morrigan's most well-known, and arguably main, aspects may be battle, death, and war but she also has other purviews including sovereignty and that is what many of her followers today seem to connect most strongly with. In our modern world many people feel disempowered in their lives, making the idea of reconnecting with personal power an alluring one, and something that the Morrigan can help with by pushing us to find our own sense of sovereignty. She is not, in this case, a giver of sovereignty to those who seek it, but rather she will challenge us to fight for the independence and strength we need to feel like we are in control of our own selves.

Over time the concept of sovereignty has evolved. It is no longer restricted to kings and rulers but has become something personal, something that we all have within us. Whereas the Irish word flaitheas applies very specifically to rulership, kingdoms, and domains, the English translation of sovereignty has different meanings which have come to shape our understanding. Sovereignty is not only about rulership and authority over others, but also about personal autonomy and freedom, in essence about our ability to rule over ourselves. To have personal sovereignty is to stand in our personal power, take responsibility for all of our actions and their consequences, and to embrace the idea that we are ultimately our own authority. Our bodies belong only to ourselves. Our lives are lived as we choose to live them, whether that is for ourselves or for others, for our own happiness, or for other peoples'. Personal sovereignty is a choice, even when we are in situations where we can't control or choose what is happening, we can choose how we react to the situations we are in. We each have the possibility of connecting to the goddess of sovereignty. We each have the potential for self-determination. We each have the capacity to be completely in control of ourselves and our own actions, to live by choice and not by chance, and in doing so to live in right relation to the goddess of sovereignty and earn her blessing in our life.

Just as the word itself has changed with time, so too has the purview of the goddess of sovereignty changed over time. The Morrigan is still who and what she was historically, nothing has fallen away from her, but new things have been added as the world and human society changed, because the gods grow and adapt with us. In the past she might decide who would rule by shaping the outcome of a battle, or by challenging kings to act when action was needed. Macha, a goddess who is one of the three Morrigans, was directly associated with sovereignty by blessing or cursing kings, and, as Macha Mongruadh, with choosing the king. In a modern context the Morrigan comes to us individually and provokes us to embrace our own autonomy, to find our own sense of personal sovereignty.

The Morrigan is not known as a gentle goddess although how she interacts with us can depend on the situation and the person. In inciting us to find our own sovereignty she is challenging. Like a smith separating the dross from the good material she does what is needed to make us stronger. She pushes us to confront our fears, to admit our weaknesses and turn them into strengths, to face the things we want only to avoid, to confront instead of hide. She teaches us that sovereignty has a price, but if we are willing to pay that price, she will help us become better, stronger people. She does not give anything easily or freely but she will push us to find our own way to our personal power. Because what she offers has great value it is not easily earned nor freely given, but it is more than worth the effort.

The Morrigan does not give sovereignty - she urges us to embrace our own by challenging us to find our strength and stand in our power. We may each have different definitions of what sovereignty is, but however we choose to define it we should strive to understand how it fits into our life. Decide for yourself what sovereignty is and then find a way to embrace it. The Morrigan stands before us and says: *"Who rules your life? Dare to be your own sovereign, dare to rule over your own flesh, dare to be in control of your own self."*

The Morrigan and the Idea of Mother Goddesses

This idea for this section was actually started in a conversation about the Morrigan as a mother goddess and I want to say right at the off that I have nothing against people who believe that she is. Modern worshipers see the Morrigan in diverse ways that are often deeply significant for each individual and I am in no way trying to argue against those views. You can have whatever personal relationship with any deity you feel that you have, and don't worry about whether or not those views are shared. It may not be my view, but such is life - and likewise my views and how I relate to her shouldn't be terribly upsetting to you if they don't agree with your own. Personal views and understandings by their nature will always be deeply personal and individual.

But I think it's important to have this discussion as the idea of the Morrigan as a mother goddess, like the idea of her as a sex goddess, which we will also be discussing, is sometimes taken outside the realm of personal interaction and projected onto her character more generally and that is a bit problematic. Seeing her as a mother figure to yourself is one thing; stating that she is a mother-type deity in a general sense is another.

The Morrigan is not a mother goddess in the modern neopagan sense. I am aware of books who try to fit her into a Maiden-Mother-Crone paradigm will put her, often, into the mother category but she doesn't fit into this by her nature. The idea of a triple M-M-C goddess comes to us from the 20th century, while the kinds of triple deities we find in older Irish mythology are usually sisters and act together or in activities along the same lines. With the Morrigan and her two sisters those lines are war and prophecy, while for another example with Brighid those lines would be creativity and creation (depending on how we are viewing healing).

From a purely mythological standpoint as a mother the evidence for her having children is complicated. She is said to have a son named Meiche - but he had to be killed because he had three serpents in his heart who would have grown and destroyed Ireland. The Lebor Gabala Erenn names her as the mother of a trio of sons, but that may be a case of conflating her with another goddess in an attempt to homogenize the folklore when the stories where written down. She is named as the mother of a daughter by the Dagda, but the daughter is an obscure figure who we don't know much about. She is also said to have 52 children who were warriors in the Silva Gadelica, but in context it seems likely they were actually people dedicated to her and not physical children. So. there's not much solid evidence for her as a physical mother of children and certainly not in the prodigious way of, say, Flidais who one can easily argue does fit the image of a mother goddess.

Secondly from a more Jungian viewpoint she doesn't fit the archetypal pattern of the Mother very well either. The Mother, as an archetype[1], is gentle, nurturing, caring, loving, and supportive, because she represents the idealized qualities of the concept of a mother. The Morrigan is many, many awesome and inspiring things but when I think of words to describe her "nurturing" and "gentle" don't exactly spring immediately to my mind. Not to say she can't be those things if she is in the mood to be - blackthorn can make a safe refuge for small birds avoiding predators, but that doesn't mean my first thought when it's mentioned is "cuddly" (seriously have you seen those thorns?). My point here - no pun intended, mostly - is that while I do think the Morrigan can be caring and supportive to those who honor her, I don't think occasionally acting that way or taking on that role under specific circumstances makes her the embodiment of the Mother in an archetypal way. I do think that it's a very interesting thing that so very many neopagans seem to be seeking out a Mother in the goddesses they honor, to the point of seeing that Mother and the qualities of mothering in goddesses who far more easily could be said to embody the Anti-Mother or Negative Mother.

The Morrigan to me, if I were going to describe her in a personal sense, is a force of incitement and empowerment. She can be supportive, but she also pushes me to achieve. She can be caring, but she doesn't let me slack or give excuses. She can be gentle, but she can also be brutal, harsh, and push me past what I thought was my limit so that I realize that I am stronger and braver than I realized. She can be nurturing, but she nurtures my potential by driving me to achieve and pushing me to excel. She will stand up and defend me only until the moment I can do it for myself, and she will be urging me the entire time to stand up. She does not chase away my nightmares, but teaches me to face them. That is who she is to me.

For myself, my own viewpoint is both simpler and, in a way, more complex. She just doesn't resonate with me as a mother goddess, nor as a deity, quite frankly, of sex, nor of fertility[2] although these are all popular views of her. I don't see her as a goddess of rebirth or birth either - although I'll repeat here that if you do, that's fine, I'm not trying to attack anyone else's opinions, just to share my own thoughts. To me a mother Goddess is about more than fiercely protecting your children or family - after all isn't that what most warriors are doing? Wasn't that why the pleas of Cu Chulainn's father, Súaltaim, during the Táin Bó Cúailnge to arouse the Ulstermen to fight include saying "your wives and sons and children are taken"? I feel like being fiercely protective speaks more to her warrior side than anything else, to the desire and ability to fight for what needs to be fought for. What makes her a goddess of fertility? Being female and connected to sex? So far no one has been able to offer an actual explanation beyond a tenuous argument that as Anu if she's connected to the earth, she is by default a fertility goddess, to which I would ask everyone to consider - what defines a fertility goddess? For me personally a fertility deity is someone I pray to for physical fertility of myself, my animals, and my crops and while I may ask the Morrigan to increase my cattle via successful raiding she just isn't who I would go to for physical fertility (which again isn't to say she might not answer someone for that if she felt like it, she's a goddess she can influence whatever she wants to). No mythic associations, no folklore, so just not something I see as her bailiwick. The same arguments hold true for re-birth and birth.

I'll emphasize again - and again and again - though that just because a deity is generally most strongly associated with something doesn't mean that they are limited to those things. To use a rough analogy, the Morrigan can be a goddess of war, battle, and death but may also choose to relate to an individual in a unique way, just as a person can specialize in a skill but also be able to do other things they have no training in. I think where it starts to get messy is when someone has a personal association with a deity and then associates that outwards into a generalization for everyone. Also, I know some people really dislike the idea of a deity being the "goddess of ----" because they find it limiting to that deity, but it's pretty clear looking at both ancient pagan religions and modern ones that deities have always specialized. If you look at Hinduism, Santeria, any tribal religion, Egyptian paganism, Hellenismos, Shinto, and so on some gods were always worshiped for certain things and other gods for other things - the idea of any one deity doing it all is very uncommon. I might even venture to say that the idea of an interactive, all-powerful, all-influential, all-encompassing deity in a polytheistic sense is very post-modern but I'm sure someone will find an example to contradict me.

I'm not always very good at binary thinking, and this is an example of where my perspective varies because I just don't see the Morrigan as defined, in any significant way, by her vagina. Yes, she's a goddess. Yes, she's female. Yes, she in many ways exemplifies female empowerment. But I just can't bring myself to see her as defined by those features which make her female - her ability to give birth, her ability to have sex, her ability to mother - these are all part of her but only in a modern context have they become aspects which we focus on and emphasize. And in some cases, in some contexts I have seen them emphasized in ways that reduce her to just another overly-sexualized woman in a culture that doesn't respect women very much. I've seen male devotees talk about her as if she was their girlfriend or some sort of anime fantasy, emphasizing only her sex and fertility aspects; and that does make me uncomfortable and more than a bit offended. I've seen female devotees talk about her as if she was nothing but gentle and loving kindness, the perfect mother fulfilling that fantasy for them. And maybe she is those things to those people, because maybe that's what they need, or maybe she isn't and they just see what they want to see, I have no idea, and I honestly can say it's between Her and them. But I just can't see Her in those ways. To me she will always be powerful and awesome - awe inspiring - not because she is female but because she is Herself.

The Morrigan, Sex, and the Idea of a Sex Goddess

Let me repeat that we all see the Gods differently and I know that sometimes a person can relate to a deity in a way that is unusual (comparatively) or unique to them; maybe this is how they need to see that deity for personal reasons. What I want to address here is something that I've seen more and more often among people discussing the Morrigan, and that is the idea that she is a goddess of sex or sexuality - not that an individual relates to her that way but that it is a definitive part of who she, as a deity, is. People even claim that it is one of her main purviews. I've seen it said in many places by many different people, and in a wider way we can see it reflected in the way she is often shown in artwork: scantily clad (or nude), alluringly posed, oozing sex appeal even on a battlefield or among corpses.

I won't address the way she appears in statues here, as that gets into a wider social issue. I will only say that I don't think clothes or lack of clothes is the problem. I love Paul Borda's Morrigan statue, which depicts her nude and as a warrior. I don't find it sexy at all or male gaze oriented and I think that's the key. One can be naked and powerful or one can be naked and vulnerable, and too often the 'nude Morrigan' artwork shows her as the latter. And I'm sorry people but when she's being shown looking like a very young woman who couldn't physically hold the blade she's carrying - or is holding it point down over her own foot! - it's pretty clear that the image isn't meant to depict a powerful goddess but simply an attractive female body. What I want to discuss here is why, exactly, this idea of the Morrigan as a goddess of sexuality and sex is problematic to me and why it concerns me to see it spreading.

One of the most often repeated things I run across is the idea that the Morrigan has lots of lovers among the gods, or her stories are full of sexual trysts with gods and mortals. So, let's start by looking at the Morrigan's mythology and when and how often she has sexual encounters. Don't worry this won't take long.

The Cath Maige Tuired:

The Dagda had a house at Glenn Etin in the north. The Dagda was to meet a woman on a day, yearly, about Samain of the battle at Glen Etin. The Unish of Connacht calls by the south. The woman was at the Unish of Corand washing her genitals, one of her two feet by Allod Echae, that is Echumech, by water at the south, her other by Loscondoib, by water at the north. Nine plaits of hair undone upon her head. The Dagda speaks to her and they make a union. Bed of the Married Couple was the name of that place from then. She is the Morrigan, the woman mentioned particularly here. (translation my own)

Táin Bó Cúailnge:

"Cú Chulainn saw coming towards him a young woman of surpassing beauty, clad in clothes of many colours.

'Who are you?' asked Cú Chulainn.

'I am the daughter of Búan the king,' said she. 'I have come to you for I fell in love with you on hearing your fame, and I have brought with me my treasures and my cattle.'

'It is not a good time at which you have come to us, that is, our condition is ill, we are starving. So, it is not easy for me to meet a woman while I am in this strife.'

'I shall help you in it.'

'It is not for a woman's body that I have come.'

'It will be worse for you', said she, 'when I go against you as you are fighting your enemies. I shall go in the form of an eel under your feet in the ford so that you shall fall.'

'I prefer that to the king's daughter,' said he.'"

- Táin Bó Cúailnge, Recension 1, O Rahilly translation

So, there you go. That's it. In the first example we see the Morrigan and the Dagda having a pre-arranged meeting at a set time and place, and it should be noted that the two are likely married. The reference above notes this when it says the place they lay together was called 'the Bed of the Married Couple' and the Morrigan is called the Dagda's wife in other sources like the Metrical Dindshenchas. In the second example - which please note does not occur in all version of the Táin Bó Cúailnge - we see the Morrigan approaching Cu Chulainn disguised as a young woman and proclaiming her love for him. I am highly suspicious, as are several scholars, of the genuineness of this and believe it is most likely a trick to try to get him to abandon the ford he is guarding. Some scholars have suggested this bit of narrative was added later by scribes unfamiliar with the Táin Bó Regamna who needed an explanation for why the Morrigan then set herself against Cu Chulainn. In any event as you can see, she never actually offers him sex or tries to seduce him, although she does offer her love and her goods as what would have been either a wife or as a mistress.

In fairness I will add that there is, as far as I'm aware, one description of Herself appearing naked, from the Cath Magh Rath:

Bloody over his head, fighting, crying out
A naked hag, swiftly leaping
Over the edges of their armor and shields
She is the grey-haired Morrigu
(translation mine)

In this text the Morrigan is specifically described as grey-haired and a hag, and is leaping over an army about to engage in battle, shrieking.

Why then is it repeated so often that the Morrigan is a sexual goddess and has multiple sexual encounters?

At this point I think a lot of it is simply the internet effect, where one website stated it as a fact at some point[3] and now it gets repeated and passed on as fact. The idea appeals to people for different reasons. In my own experience I have found that some men like the idea of the Morrigan as a goddess of sex and as sexual because it allows them to relate to her the way they would to a beautiful human woman. I have seen some women like this idea because they find it sexually empowering for themselves. There is also, of course, the fact that in video games and fiction she's shown as sexual and sex focused, and while those are fiction and entertainment, we can't underestimate the way that does impact how people start to subconsciously relate to the deity.

That all sounds like it could be good, but it concerns me on a couple levels. Firstly, while I do appreciate the desire for women to feel sexually empowered and to look to a goddess as a role model here, reshaping the Morrigan to do it is only reinforcing existing Western ideas of beauty and female power - we focus on the Morrigan as a young beautiful woman who is powerful because she engages in sexual relationships with men on her own terms. That seems great on the surface, sure, but what about seeing her as beautiful as the naked hag? As the red-haired satirist? As a crow or raven? What about seeing her as powerful without a man? Or simply acknowledging her power as a goddess of battle, incitement, prophecy, and sovereignty? Basically, my question is why do we have to make her into something she isn't when she already is beautiful and powerful in a different way?

The other side of that coin, the objectification, is a more complicated problem. It seems to me to rest not on redefining her power but on reducing it by taking a fearsome goddess of several things that are genuinely terrifying for humans and making her into a deity of things humans find pleasant and enjoyable. Instead of a deity of war and death she becomes a goddess of sexual pleasure; instead of a screaming hag above armies she becomes a young girl with come-hither eyes and scanty clothing. And to me that speaks volumes about containing her power by limiting her to ideas and to an image that our culture sees as both safe and inherently disempowered.

Yes, gods evolve and change with their worshippers, but that change in the past was usually organic and a slow process. We live in a world now where a single person can assert something as fact and that assertion, based in nothing but one person's opinion, can then spread quickly and far as fact - and that in my opinion is not how the evolution of gods has ever worked before. When we take a being with history and depth and layers of mythology and detach them from their own stories and personality and make them nothing more than a mirror for our own desires, we aren't engaging with deity anymore, whether we see deity as archetype or as unique individual beings. Perhaps in time there will be a new deity - a new version - of the older goddess created from this milieu of rootless belief. But it will not be the Morrigan of Irish culture, it will be something created from modern beauty standards and sexual mores. And we need to be aware of that and of what that really means.

The Morrigan isn't, in my opinion, a good candidate for a sex deity - but then who is? Well, I think when we look at the Irish pantheon the Dagda as sex god makes a lot of sense. But I also think that all the same cultural reasons why we, collectively, want to force this title into the Morrigan are the same reasons we avoid it for the Dagda. When we make a powerful female figure sexier, we make her safer, particularly when we are using imagery and language that hinges on defining her by roles our society sees as weaker. When we make a male figure more sexually imposing though one of two things happens: its comedic or its frightening. The Dagda is a physically big figure, a warrior, powerful - the idea of his being a sex deity may frighten some people. He is also often mislabeled as an 'all father'[4] deity and envisioned as a kind of red-haired, portly Santa-type and our culture really dislikes seeing that as sexy, we'd much rather find comedy in it. And that is also something I think we should give some serious thought to.

People are always free to hold their own opinions. I have

shared mine here, and my reasoning for why I think and feel as I do. The Morrigan is not a sex goddess for me, or a goddess of sex or sexuality. But she is fierce, and beautiful, and powerful. She is a goddess of personal autonomy and of the sovereignty of kings. She is the land, blood soaked after battle, and the shrieking cry of warriors plunging blade-first into conflict. She is the voice that inspires the downtrodden to rise up and fight for freedom, and the whispers of prophecy foretelling the fate of all. She is awesome in the oldest sense of the word. And that is enough.

Thoughts on The Morrigan, Service, and Diversity

I want to end this chapter with some thoughts on the value of diversity in the community of modern Morrigan worshippers.

I think it's important to always remember that no single approach will work for everyone. Also, something we all should give more thought to, not only in the general sense that each tradition won't be right for everyone - Gods know recon isn't for everyone - but also that even those who are dedicated to the same deity will find different expressions of that dedication. We each have our own niches within our service. Perhaps we can say that there are often themes within the things people who share a deity are drawn to, commonalities, but each of us finds our own expression. We are each filled with a different passion. It's easy to forget though that those who honor the same deity we honor do not necessarily share the calling that drives us.

I have only rarely met other people dedicated to Macha, but I know many more generally dedicated to the Morrigan. I see the expression of the things that drive them and sometimes I nod in agreement and sometimes I shake my head or shrug. The things that they are so profoundly driven by may or may not be things that I understand or share. In the same way the things that drive me are not the things that drive them. I know many honorable Morrigan's people who have taken up wonderful causes in Her name, including things like raising money to donate to charities like the Wounded Warrior Project. I admire that, but it is not my cause to carry forward.

I have a deep concern for the welfare of children, especially infants and for the rights of parents to provide care. I'm a pretty outspoken against circumcision and strongly advocate breastfeeding rights[5], for example. In fact, the only social protest I've participated in was a "nurse-in" that came about after a woman was asked to stop nursing at a local restaurant. I have helped with fundraisers in my area to donate to the local women's shelter and to food pantries. I don't tie those things directly into my dedication to Macha, but I certainly have come to feel over the years that She is a deity who is very much about justice for women and children[6]. When I think of serving Macha, I can't help but think as well of speaking up in defense of the helpless, especially children, and of defending mother's rights. I feel like that's part of my personal calling. But I have to remind myself that just because these things matter to me doesn't mean they matter to others, not even other people who serve Her. It would be unfair of me to judge others for not sharing in the drive I feel to fight for these things. Instead I try to see and appreciate the things they do want to fight for.

Some of us are called to write and teach while others sing, or dance, or live quiet lives of devotion. Some of us feel very passionate about a cause, others don't. We are a diverse group, a wide array of people from different walks of life and places - in every sense - who all seek to honor the Morrigan. As tempting as it can be to want to measure everyone by our own standard, we need to let go of the idea of expecting everybody to be like us, to share our goals and ideals. Our service takes many different forms, and we should strive to appreciate the service offered by others, as much as we work at doing the best on our own path.

End Notes

1 A Jungian archetype that is - the word gets tossed around

a lot in neopaganism but I honestly don't understand how it's being used about half the time. In Jungian psychology as I understand it, an archetype is an unconscious, inherited idea of the ideal pattern or type of a thing that humans get form the collective unconscious and which is shared across cultures. So hence the archetypal Hero, Mother, and Trickster. Archetypes aren't decided by individuals but are dictated by the sum total of human experience and cultural inheritance.

2   Macha, however, is arguably a fertility goddess something I discuss in my article "Macha, Horses, and Sovereignty" which can be found in the 2015 anthology "Grey Mare on the Hill".

3   This is exactly how the idea that falcons are connected to her and that she is a goddess of rebirth happened. One website more than a decade ago, run by someone who was very honest that they were posting channeled and personal material said it, and it spread from there. Once it was accepted into the common belief no one really knew where it had come from or why they believed it.

4   Ollathair doesn't mean all father but great or ample father. It certainly connects him to abundance but not to physical proliferation.

5   Every woman must feed her child in the way that is best for them, and I do not judge what way that is, but I am a strong proponent for the right of anyone to feed a child anywhere at any time, and in the support of a person's legal rights to nurse uncovered in public.

6   This has grown out of my contemplation of her cursing the men of Ulster, although I do realize that story has a lot of other layers as well.

Chapter 7

Ways to Feel More Connected

One question that I am asked on a fairly regular basis is what should people who are interested in connecting spiritually to the Morrigan or who are just beginning to honor Her do? I wanted to end this book by looking at this topic, although keep in mind that these are only my ideas and what I have found works well for me. I tend to be a very sensory person so you'll note a lot of this involves sensory experiences - sound, sight, touch - and that may appeal to some people and not to others. These suggestions are meant to be tailored to you personally, so please take them and play with them to find what works best for yourself.

Myths and Stories

The very first thing I'll suggest is to read as many of the old myths and stories as you can, preferably as close to the originals as possible. The re-tellings are nice – obviously I've included some of my own in this book – but many like Lady Gregory's *Gods and Fighting Men* take liberties with the stories and change details that make big differences. This is something you need to be aware of when weighing the value of a source.

I'm always going to be an advocate for going to the source material itself. You can find many of the older stories at Mary Jones *Celtic Literature Collective* and the stories which feature the Morrigan include the Cath Mag Tuired Cunga, Cath Maige Tuired, Lebor Gabala Erenn, and many of the tales in the Ulster Cycle.

Beyond that there are several modern authors who have written in detail about the Morrigan that are worth reading - my favorite is Angelique Gulermovich Epstein's *War Goddess: The Morrigan and Her Germano-Celtic Counterparts*.

Locations

If possible, you should go and visit the places the stories happen in. Smell the air, touch the earth, feel the wind. Stand in the places that the Morrigan herself is said to have stood in, is still said to stand in, like Uaimh na gCat, and feel her presence there. Below I'm going to list a selection of the more well-known or easily accessible sites you may consider, but understand these are not the only possibilities. The Morrigan has many different sites associated with her.

The River Unshin

The river Unshin is the place where it's said, at a ford of this river near Samhain time, the Dagda had a yearly arrangement to meet the Morrigan. He found her straddling the water washing herself with her hair unbound from nine plaits and the two united. Afterwards the place was called 'Lige ina Lanomhnou' which means roughly 'Bed of the Married Couple'. This river is a real place and can be found in Ireland although the exact location of the ford is debated.

Dumha na nGiall

It was then that Badb and Macha and Morrigan went to the Knoll of the Taking of the Hostages, and to the Hill of Summoning of Hosts at Tara, and sent forth magic showers of sorcery and compact clouds of mist and a furious rain of fire, with a downpour of red blood from the air on the warriors' heads; and they allowed the Fir Bolg neither rest nor stay for three days and nights. - Cet-Chath Maige Tuired

Dumha na nGiall [mound of hostages] is a 5,000-year-old passage tomb at Teamhair [Tara] at the edge of the section known as Raith na Ríg [fort of kings]. The mound is built in the same way as most other passage tombs and includes some beautiful, intricate carving of the stones at the entrance. The mound was actively used for burials for a thousand years and had up to 500 cremated remains in it. The entrance is now blocked with a heavy iron grate but you can still look inside somewhat. This is the location mentioned in the above quote, where the Morrigan, Badb, and Macha went and worked magic against the Fir Bolg when the Tuatha De Danann had first come to Ireland.

Bru na Boinne

There are multiple locations of importance in the Bru na Boinne complex, but of note here is a reference to the 'Bed of the Couple' in the Dindshenchas Bru na Boinde I:

Here slept a married pair
after the battle of Mag Tuired yonder,
the great lady and the swart Dagda:
not obscure is their dwelling there.

It's unclear exactly where this location is within the Neolithic complex although this line from Bru na Boinde II gives us a hint:

Behold the Bed of the red Dagda:
on the slope, without rough rigour

This description comes immediately after one of Sidhe in Broga [Newgrange] and before one of Dá Chích na Morrígna which may also give us a hint of the location we are looking for.

Dá Chích na Morrígna

The Paps of the Morrigan are a pair of hills near the Bru na Boinne complex. They can be seen from Sidhe in Broga [Newgrange].

Cloch an Fhir Mhóir

And there [Cu Chulainn] drank his drink, and washed himself, and came forth to die, calling on his foes to come to meet him.

Now a great mearing went westwards from the loch and his eye lit upon it, and he went to a pillar-stone which is in the plain, and he put his breast-girdle round it that he might not die seated nor lying down, but that he might die standing up.

Aided Conculaind

Folklore and local tradition say that Cloch an Fhir Mhóir was the place that Cu Chulainn died at. The standing stone is located in the middle of a private field so if you do try to visit it keep in mind that the field is in active use for farming and be respectful. The stone itself is worth a visit as the location where Cu Chulainn died and therefore where the Morrigan perched either on the pillar itself or on his shoulder.

Uaimh na gCat

Uaimh na gCat, the Cave of Cats, the Cave of the Morrigan and in the Dindshenchas of Odras it is called the sidhe of Cruachan. Also called "Ireland's Hellmouth" by some. To me, after going in and coming back out again, it will always be the Sí of Cruachan but that's another story.

The cave itself, deep down and a slippery climb into the earth to reach, is a natural feature but the entrance is a man-made souterrain which makes for an odd contrast of experience going in and coming out. You ease into the earth, reaching up to touch the Ogham carved on the lintel, and the first dozen feet in is all hard lines and sharp edges - it feels man made. It feels carved. And then that transition point and you leave behind the hand of man and move into the sections made by nature, and it just feels different. Smoother, even where its jagged. Everything here is all wet clay that sucks and clings, as if the cave means to keep you. And maybe it does. But you go anyway, into the darkness that only the deep earth can have, where sunlight has never even been a dream. And maybe you understand why people describe caves as wombs, or maybe you understand why darkness drives some people mad or terrifies them, or maybe down there you find Herself waiting. And that's the cave.

If it's not possible to physically visit these places then quiet meditation wherever you are is good, but I am I do encourage people if it's possible to go to Ireland and visit the sites firsthand. Even if it's a once in a lifetime goal there is a difference between reading about places and actually experiencing them. Until then of course you can do your best to feel connected to the locations of the myths, to the places where the Gods are invested in the land itself by learning as much as possible about them. And if it's not possible at all for whatever reason then pictures, videos, or meditation are viable alternatives.

Shrines

Set up a small shrine to her. I'm a fan of statues and artwork and there is a huge amount to choose from for the Morrigan. My favorite statue is Dryad Design's Morrigan, which I bought and then painted myself. There are also a variety of great art prints out there. Beyond that personalize as you see fit. I like shrines because they provide a quiet place to sit and visually reflect on the Gods, as well as being a place to light candles, burn incense, and make offerings.

Offerings

Speaking of making offerings. A good way to establish a connection to any deity is to begin making offerings to them. For the Morrigan my own preferences are milk (or cream), whiskey, or bread, although I often offer different things spontaneously as well if I feel drawn to.

Prayer

This tends to be less popular with some people but it really is a good way to connect. Whatever works best for you, whether that's formal memorized prayers or spontaneous speaking from the heart, the point is just to reach out and speak to the Gods.

Playlist

I also encourage people to make their own custom playlist of music about the Morrigan or of songs that remind you of her. There are a surprising number of songs about the Morrigan these days that you can check out on YouTube and also a wider array of music that may make you think of her even she's not the intended theme. I really love music as a vehicle for altered states, trancework, and just plain feeling more strongly connected to something. When it comes to the Morrigan my personal favorites are Omnia's 'Morrigan', Darkest Era's 'The Morrigan', Heather Dale's 'The Morrigan', and Cruachan's 'Brown Bull of Cooley' and 'The Morrigan's Call'. I've found that it's really helpful for me in feeling more connected to her to have this sort of resource and it's something that you can truly personalize however you like it.

Jewelry

My final suggestion would be to get a piece of jewelry that represents or symbolizes the Morrigan for you, that you can wear to help you feel more connected to her. This is largely a psychological thing for the person, a physical token to touch when you need that tactile reminder. Over time though it can become sacred in its own right as its blessed or empowered.

* * *

There you go, a short basic list but one that I find effective. Many or most of these may just be common sense but I have found they are all helpful, especially if done regularly. Having a regular spiritual practice is vital in my opinion and this is how I incorporate the Morrigan into that.

Conclusion

We began with a poem written from a dream. Let us end together with an experience, shared in what could be used as a guided meditation.

Uaimh na gCat

The entrance is in a field, beneath a hawthorn. It is an unassuming opening into the earth, but there is something intimidating about it. The darkness beyond the stone and grass is deep and full. It invites you in at the same time that it warns you away. But this is why you have come to this place, seeking this cave, seeking this darkness, and you won't be deterred now.

You move into the liminal space of the entrance, pausing and turning to look back at the light you are leaving behind. Above you there is a stone lintel, carved with ogham. Looking up your eyes trace the lines, the stone clear even in the dim light.. Then, resolved, you turn away from the world above and begin descending into a different world.

The stone path is not easy but clearly bears the marks of human hands. At first. Your feet feel for steps carved into the passageway, your hands sliding along the walls. The darkness around you is so complete and solid it fills you and becomes part of your existence. It is a living thing, coiling around you, pulling you deeper.

In this place you can't rely on sight so your other senses lead you. You touch the walls and feel with your feet. You smell the fullness of the air. You taste moisture and earth on your tongue as you breath. You hear your own movements but also the dripping of water, and the stillness which is its own sound.

Everything is damp and slick and there is a sense of subtle peril. As you move downwards the man-made steps give way to rough rock and you feel the pattern of the path changing beneath your feet, even through thick soled boots. The darkness is different here, thicker, heavier, alive.

The downward journey levels out and you are walking flat now, the space expanding out around you as you enter the cave itself. It is cool here, and damp; the walls are wet and the air you breath in feels like some greater being's exhalation. The floor is inches of clay mud that grab at you and try to hold you in place, making every step forward a battle. Nonetheless you move forward, crossing the main section of the cave until you reach the far side where it begins to climb again before leveling off and disappearing into stone. The mud is like a living thing, moving with you, around you, on you.

You are still now, hands and legs muddy, leaning into the stone wall, feeling the darkness as it encompasses you. It has its own pulse, its own rhythm, and standing there you become part of it, enveloped by it. There is a voice in that darkness that speaks to you, and you listen.

You listen.

When you finally re-emerge into the world above you are not the same.

Appendix A

Online Morrigan Resources

I want to offer personal recommendations for online accessible resources for the Morrigan, to further help people looking for more material. None of these are necessarily blanket endorsements but these are resources that can be found online, are free, and are worth reading. As with anything else in life remember to use critical thinking and to keep in mind that on this subject there can be a variety of opinions.

Dissertations and Papers - There are some great academic works out there on the Morrigan worth checking out. There are also some that I don't entirely agree with but still recommend because they add important layers to any discussion about this complex deity/ deities.

War-goddesses, furies and scald crows: The use of the word badb in early Irish literature by Kim Heijda.

The 'Mast' of Macha: The Celtic Irish and the War Goddess of Ireland by Catherine Mowat.

War Goddess: The Morrigan and Her Germano-Celtic Counterparts by Angelique Gulermovich Epstein.

Demonology, allegory and translation: the Furies and the Morrigan by Michael Clarke.

The 'Terror of the Night' and the Morrígain: Shifting Faces of the Supernatural by Jacqueline Borsje.

Blogs - There are a lot of people who blog about the Morrigan these days and I will admit my own suggestions will be limited to people I know, and read regularly. I don't go out looking around for new Morrigan bloggers because I just don't have time. You'll also note this only includes written blogs, which isn't an intentional snub to vloggers or youtubers just a reflection that I hardly ever have time to watch videos on my pc so I can't recommend them.

Dark Goddess Musings - the blog of author Stephanie Woodfield. Not updated regularly, but has interesting content http://darkgoddessmusings.blogspot.com/

Lora O'Brien - Author and Freelance Writer - what it says on the tin. Not Morrigan specific but there are Morrigan posts to be found and Lora's writing is always good and worth reading. Lora also offers paid courses on the Morrigan and several other related topics that I highly recommend. https://loraobrien.ie/blog/

Under the Ancient Oaks - the blog of Druid and author John Beckett. Not Morrigan exclusive either, but she is a frequent topic. https://www.patheos.com/blogs/johnbeckett/2017/07/hear-call-morrigan.html

Websites - An assortment of Morrigan related websites out there that I am aware of and whose content is generally reliable.

Scath na Feannoige - Morrigan content and content focused on the warrior path. Some free and some paid access, but excellent material. http://www.dunsgathan.net/feannog/index.htm

Mary Jones Celtic Literature Collective - as advertised, a resource for all things Celtic. Your best source for myths on the Morrigan (in the Irish lit section) and also offering an encyclopedia section http://www.ancienttexts.org/library/celtic/ctexts/index_irish.html

Story Archaeology - A great resource for newer translations of the myths and discussion of the stories in context. If you search the site/podcast you'll find multiple results relating to the Morrigan http://storyarchaeology.com/tag/the-morrigan/

Coru Cathubodua - a site by a group dedicated to the Morrigan, with articles and a resource list http://www.corupriesthood.com/the-morrigan/

Artwork - Some of my personal favorite sources for Morrigan artwork I like. Artwork is of course very personal so you may or may not like my suggestions, but either way I encourage you to seek out Morrigan art that speaks to you. I can't list Morrigan resources without including some art, but of course these aren't free.

The Ever Living Ones, art of Jane Brideson - http://theeverlivingones.blogspot.com/p/gallery-of-goddesses.html

Ashley Bryner - https://www.etsy.com/listing/114345068/phantom-queen?ref=shop_home_active_3

Gemma Zoe Jones - http://www.gemmazoejones.com/gallery/2016/11/25/the-morrigan

Emily Brunner - https://www.emilybrunner.com/store/morrigan-13

Valerie Herron - http://www.valerieherron.com/illustrations.html

Dryad Design - statuary and jewelry by Paul Borda - https://dryaddesign.com/small-morrigan-statue/

Books - I should probably mention here that generally I am not aware of any decent books on the Morrigan, specifically, that are available *free* online. You can access some older public domain works including Hennessey's *War Goddess* on Sacred Texts but books that old have issues with some seriously outdated scholarship and need to be read with a large grain of salt. They are worth reading with some critical thinking and discernment but I wouldn't give them a blanket recommendation.

Bibliography

Bannshenchus, (n.d.)

Carey, J., (2014) A London Library, An Irish Manuscript, A British Myth? The Wanderings of 'The Battle of Moytirra'

Dunn, J., (1914) Tain Bo Cualgne

Gray, E., (1983) Cath Maige Tuired

Green, M., (1992). Animals in Celtic Life and Myth

Gulermovich Epstein, A., (1998). War Goddess: The Morrígan and her Germano-Celtic Counterparts. Electronic version, #148, September, (1998). Retrieved from http://web.archive.org/web/20010616084231/members.loop.com/~musofire/diss/

Gwynne, E., (1906) Metrical Dindshenchas

Heijda, K, (2007). War-Goddesses, Furies, and Scald Crows: the use of the word badb in early Irish literature

Jones, H., (1997) Concerning the Names Morgan, Morgana, Morgaine, Muirghein, Morrigan and the Like. Retrieved from https://medievalscotland.org/problem/names/morgan.shtml

Kelly, F., (2005). A Guide to Early Irish Law

Macalister, R., (1940). Lebor Gabala Erenn

MacCana, P., (1992) Laíded, Gressacht 'Formalized Incitement'

MacKillop, J., (2006) Dictionary of Celtic Mythology

Martin, W., (1895). Pagan Ireland an Archaeological Sketch

Morgan la Fay (2018) The Camelot Project; University of Rochester. Retrieved from http://www.kingarthursknights.com/others/morganlefay.asp

O Donaill, N., (1977). Focloir Gaeilge-Bearla

O hOgain, D., (1991). Myth, Legend, and Romance

--- (2006) The Lore of Ireland

O'Mulconry's Glossary (n.d.) http://www.asnc.cam.ac.uk/irishglossaries/

Ó Néill, J., (2003). Lapidibus in igne calefactis coquebatur: The Historical Burnt Mound ‹Tradition›

O Tuathail, S., (1993). The Excellence of Ancient word: Druid Rhetoric from Ancient Irish Tales

Royal Irish Academy (1870). Proceedings of the Royal Irish Academy

Sanas Cormaic (n.d.) http://www.asnc.cam.ac.uk/irishglossaries/

Stokes, W., (1891). Cath Maige Tuired

Windisch, E., (1905). Táin Bó Cúailnge

**MOON
BOOKS**

PAGANISM & SHAMANISM

What is Paganism? A religion, a spirituality, an alternative belief
system, nature worship? You can find support for all these definitions (and many more) in dictionaries, encyclopaedias, and text
books of religion, but subscribe to any one and the truth will evade
you. Above all Paganism is a creative pursuit, an encounter with
reality, an exploration of meaning and an expression of the soul.
Druids, Heathens, Wiccans and others, all contribute their insights
and literary riches to the Pagan tradition. Moon Books invites you
to begin or to deepen your own encounter, right here, right now.
If you have enjoyed this book, why not tell other readers by
posting a review on your preferred book site.

Recent bestsellers from Moon Books are:

Journey to the Dark Goddess
How to Return to Your Soul
Jane Meredith
Discover the powerful secrets of the Dark Goddess and
transform your depression, grief and pain into healing
and integration.
Paperback: 978-1-84694-677-6 ebook: 978-1-78099-223-5

Shamanic Reiki
Expanded Ways of Working with Universal Life Force Energy
Llyn Roberts, Robert Levy
Shamanism and Reiki are each powerful ways of healing; together,
their power multiplies. *Shamanic Reiki* introduces techniques to
help healers and Reiki practitioners tap ancient healing wisdom.
Paperback: 978-1-84694-037-8 ebook: 978-1-84694-650-9

Pagan Portals – The Awen Alone
Walking the Path of the Solitary Druid
Joanna van der Hoeven
An introductory guide for the solitary Druid, *The Awen Alone* will
accompany you as you explore, and seek out your own place
within the natural world.
Paperback: 978-1-78279-547-6 ebook: 978-1-78279-546-9

A Kitchen Witch's World of Magical Herbs & Plants
Rachel Patterson
A journey into the magical world of herbs and plants, filled with
magical uses, folklore, history and practical magic. By popular
writer, blogger and kitchen witch, Tansy Firedragon.
Paperback: 978-1-78279-621-3 ebook: 978-1-78279-620-6

Medicine for the Soul
The Complete Book of Shamanic Healing
Ross Heaven
All you will ever need to know about shamanic healing and how to
become your own shaman...
Paperback: 978-1-78099-419-2 ebook: 978-1-78099-420-8

Shaman Pathways – The Druid Shaman
Exploring the Celtic Otherworld
Danu Forest
A practical guide to Celtic shamanism with exercises and
techniques as well as traditional lore for exploring the Celtic
Otherworld.
Paperback: 978-1-78099-615-8 ebook: 978-1-78099-616-5

Traditional Witchcraft for the Woods and Forests
A Witch's Guide to the Woodland with Guided Meditations and
Pathworking
Mélusine Draco
A Witch's guide to walking alone in the woods, with guided
meditations and pathworking.
Paperback: 978-1-84694-803-9 ebook: 978-1-84694-804-6

Naming the Goddess
Trevor Greenfield
Naming the Goddess is written by over eighty adherents and
scholars of Goddess and Goddess Spirituality.
Paperback: 978-1-78279-476-9 ebook: 978-1-78279-475-2

Shapeshifting into Higher Consciousness
Heal and Transform Yourself and Our World with Ancient
Shamanic and Modern Methods
Llyn Roberts
Ancient and modern methods that you can use every day to
transform yourself and make a positive difference in the world.
Paperback: 978-1-84694-843-5 ebook: 978-1-84694-844-2

Readers of ebooks can buy or view any of these bestsellers by
clicking on the live link in the title. Most titles are published in
paperback and as an ebook. Paperbacks are available in traditional
bookshops. Both print and ebook formats are available online.

Find more titles and sign up to our readers' newsletter at
http://www.johnhuntpublishing.com/paganism
Follow us on Facebook at https://www.facebook.com/MoonBooks
and Twitter at https://twitter.com/MoonBooksJHP